MECHANIC MACHINE TOOL MAINTENANCE SECOND YEAR MCQ

OBJECTIVE QUESTION ANSWERS

MANOJ DOLE

Digitization is the need of the time. In the future, training in industrial training institutes will need to be conducted using online internet to make training more convenient and easy. E-books containing a set of MCQ questions will be made available to the trainees as they need to be more accustomed to the multiple choice questions MCQ to prepare for the online exams taking place in their industrial training institutes.

With all these factors in mind, Mr. Manoj Madhukar Dole Instructor, Industrial Training Institute, Satara, has written books according to the new annual system and NSQF-5 syllabus. And they've created theoretical mobile apps and blogs to make training easier, and made all these educational materials available for download on the world famous websites Google Play Store, Amazon and Apple Book Store.

The books were published by Hon'ble Joint Director Shri Rajendra Ghume Saheb Regional Office of Vocational Education and Training, Pune on 9/1/2019, at this time Shri Prakash Saigavkar Saheb Principal Government Industrial Training Institute Aundh Pune, Shri Tukaram Misal Saheb Principal Govt. Q. Sanstha Satara, Shri Sachin Dhumal Saheb District Vocational Education and Training Officer Satara, Shri Yatin Pargaonkar Saheb Principal Govt. Q. Sanstha Kolhapur, Shri Vikas Teke Saheb Inspector Vocational Education and Training Regional Office Pune, Palekar Foods Products Pvt. Ltd. Entrepreneurial Chairman of Satara Mr. Nilkanthrao Palekar Saheb, Chairman of Hira Foods Mr. Ibrahim Baba Tamboli Saheb, Mrs. Shalmali Pawar Headmaster Government Technical School Center Satara and other dignitaries were present on the occasion.

Contents

Prologue

Mechanic Machine Tool Maintenance B is a simple e-Book for ITI Engineering Course Mechanic Machine Tool Maintenance (MMTM) , Second Year, Sem- 3 & 4, Revised NSQ F-5 Syllabus in 2022, It contains objective questions with underlined & bold correct answers MCQ covering all topics including all about welding and gas cutting of metals, hydraulic and pneumatic system with advanced electro and pneumatic circuit making, preventive and breakdown maintenance of milling and grinding machines, electric, electronic and PLC system, CNC operation including setting operation and part programming in simulator, overhauling of hydraulic press, pumps & compressor, fault finding & breakdown maintenance of machines viz., shaper, grinding, milling machine and lots more.

We add new question answers with each new version. Please email us in case of any errors/omissions. This is arguably the largest and best e-Book for All engineering multiple choice questions and answers.

As a student you can use it for your exam prep. This e-Book is also useful for professors to refresh material.

Foreword

Vocational education and training is imparted through the Department of Vocational Education and Training through the Department of Business Education and Business Practical to supply multi-skilled artisans in line with the rapidly growing demand in the industrial sector in the 21st century. All the occupations within the institutions are important, as the trainees from these occupations develop multi-skills as per the demands of the industry.

with the noble intention of making available MCQ e-books suitable for all businesses, considering that all the examinations in all the industries in the industrial sector are conducted online and include MCQ method questions. Mr. Manoj Madhukar Dole has written a very good e-book on MCQ method as per the new annual syllabus. This e-book will definitely be a guide for all the trainees, trainee candidates, training instructors and others concerned.

The author of the book is Mr. Manoj Madhukar Dole, Instructor Gov. ITI Satara has 17 years of training experience. Written as a new annual pattern, this e-book incorporates modern digital QR Code technology to understand the layout, simple language, and simple syntax, diagrams and videos for each subject. So I am sure that this e-book will definitely be useful for in-depth study and exam practice. The work they have done is certainly commendable.

Mr. Tukaram Misal
Principal Government Industrial Training Institute Satara.

Preface

DGET New Delhi and CSTARI Kolkata have been implementing an annual pattern for all businesses in ITI since the August 2018 session. The examination system will also be changed and it will be online from this year and since all the questions are of Objective Type (MCQ), the trainees are in dire need of in-depth study. It is with this in mind that we are delighted to present the books based on the old NIMI pattern and a complete overview of the new annual pattern, and we hope that these books will be a guide for all business directors and trainees. Is.

For writing these books, Johar Awate Saheb, Principal of ITI Akluj. Former Principal of ITI Satara Saigavkar Saheb, Assistant Director Shri Chandrakant Dhekne Saheb Regional Office of Vocational Education and Training, Pune, District Vocational Education and Training Officer Sachin Dhumal Saheb and Headmaster Government Technical School Kendra Shalmali Pawar Madam and son Adhiraj Dole, mother Kusum Dole, I am very grateful to my father Madhukar Dole and wife Ashwini Dole for their special guidance and cooperation from time to time.

Also, in a very short period of time, the book was reviewed by Shri Rajendra Ghume Saheb, Joint Director, Vocational Education and Training Regional Office, Pune, for his invaluable time in publishing the book. I am sincerely grateful for their feedback.

I am grateful to the Instructor of ITI Satara for there continuous support from the very beginning of writing the book.

From this book, I consider myself blessed to have shared my thoughts on e-learning with you. I will not claim that this book is perfect, because considering the perfection, this book is an attempt and is in its infancy. They will be valuable for improvement if they are tested and suggested.

Manoj Dole
Dated 9/1/2019

Acknowledgements

The industrial training and theoretical examination system of our industrial training institutes and these changes have been accepted by the craft instructors and the trainees. Theoretical examinations conducted in your industrial training institutes are also conducted online. Since these examinations are of multiple choice MCQ method, the trainees will need to get more practice of such questions.

With all these considerations in mind, Mr. Manoj Madhukar, Director, Dole Crafts, Katari Industrial Training Institute, Satara, has done a thorough study and with his diligent work and added his keen intellect, according to the new annual system and NSQF-5 syllabus, e-book of Katari and other machine trades. -Book) and they have created mobile apps and blogs on theoretical topics to make training easier and have made all these educational materials available for download on the world famous websites Google Play Store, Amazon and Apple Book Store. Training has been made easier by creating a print version and using advanced techniques like QR Code.

All these educational materials will definitely be a guide for all the trainees for in-depth study and for the craft instructors and other concerned who are imparting vocational training.

CHAPTER ONE

Mechanic Machine Tool Maintenance Second Year MCQ Drawings

Online Test Exam
ITI Books
CNC Course
AutoCAD CAM
JOB & Apprentice
Online Theory
Computer Course
Trading Course
Web Designing
MSCIT Course
Shopping Business
Internet Business
Remotasks Course
Online Services
Top Sportsmans
Indian Army
Freedom Fighters
Top Scientists
Social Reformers
Motivational Speaker
Top Richest People
Join WhatsApp Group
Join Facebook Group
Like Facebook Page
PAN / Adhar / Licence Passport

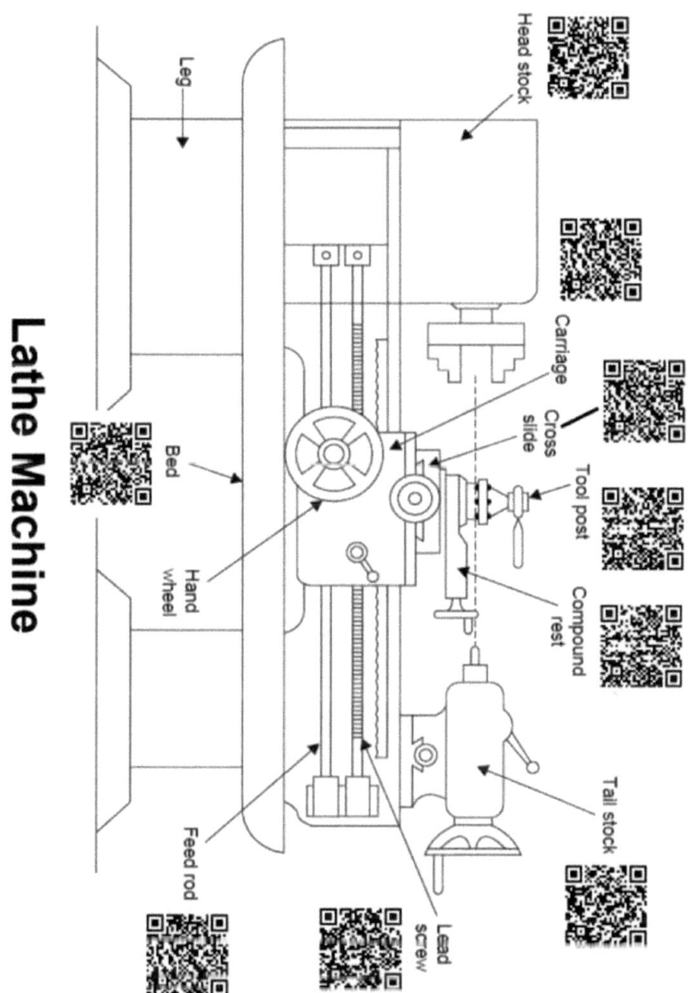
Lathe Machine
Head stock
Leg
Carriage
Cross slide
Tool post
Bed
Hand wheel
Compound rest
Tail stock
Feed rod
Lead screw

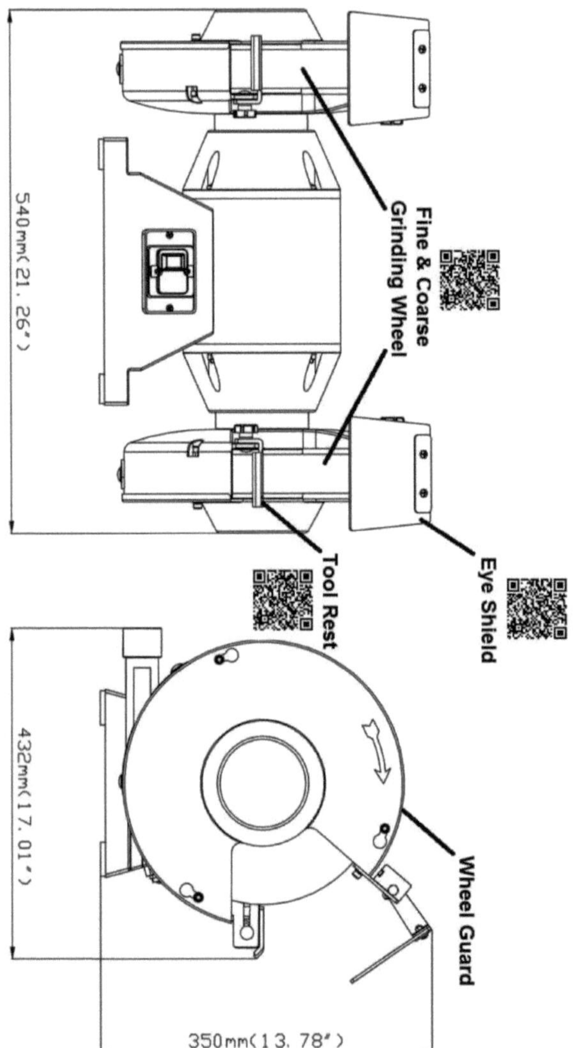
Bench Grinding Machine
Fine & Coarse Grinding Wheel
Eye Shield
Tool Rest
Wheel Guard
540mm(21.26")
432mm(17.01")
350mm(13.78")

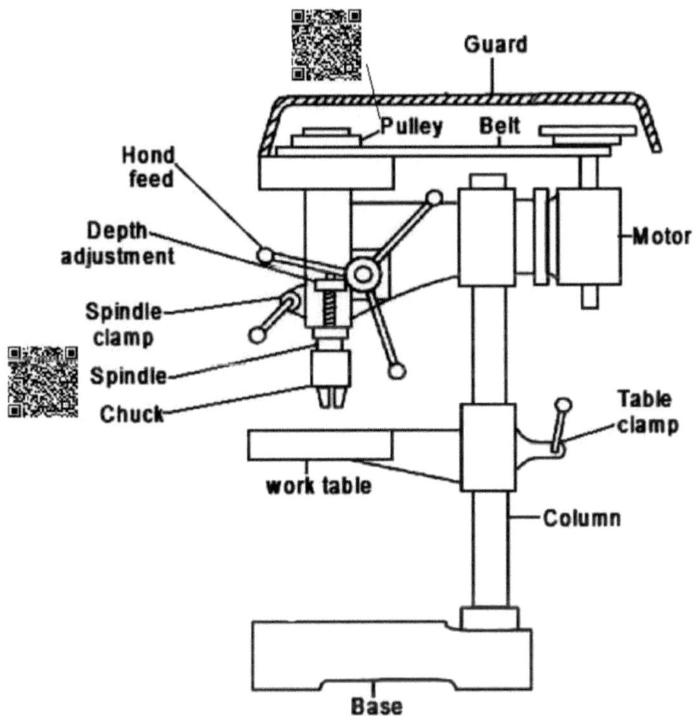

Piller Drilling Machine

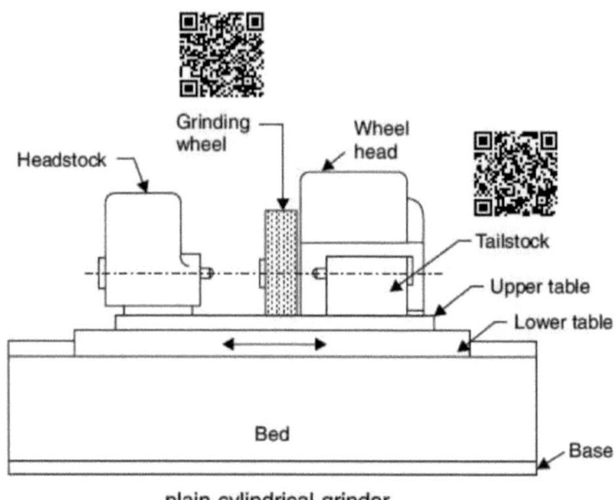

plain cylindrical grinder

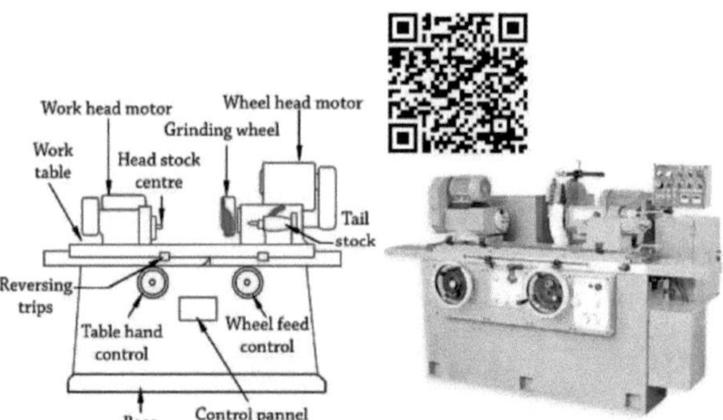

Cylindrical grinding machine

To study Different operations and parts of Surface Grinding Machine

SURFACE GRINDER

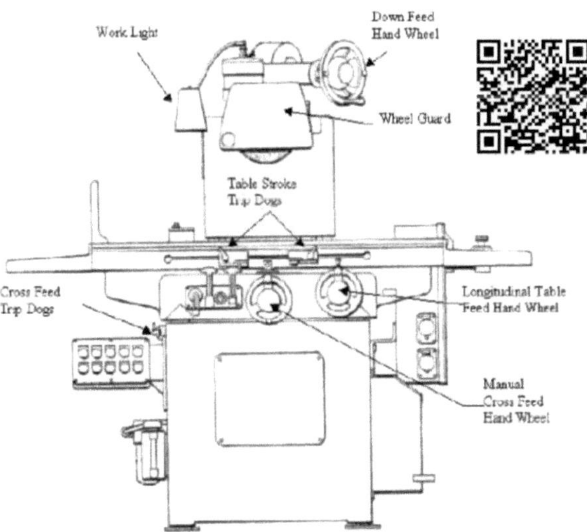

Surface grinding is used to produce a smooth finish on flat surfaces. It is a widely used abrasive machining process in which a spinning wheel covered in rough particles (grinding wheel) cuts

PLAIN OR HORIZONTAL MILLING MACHINE

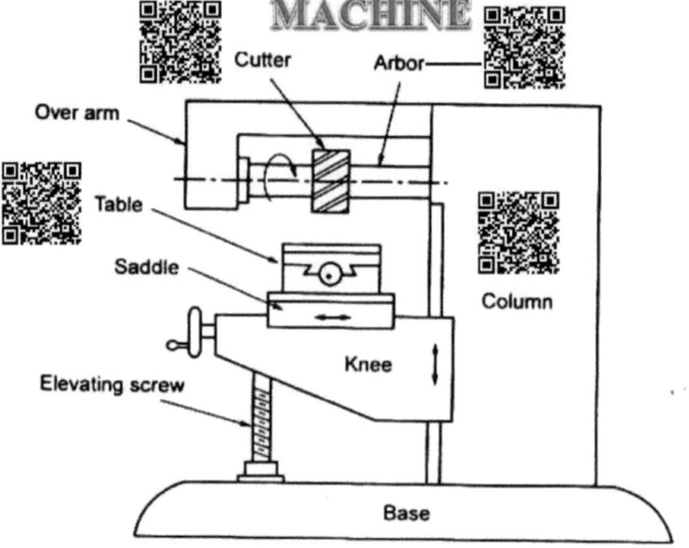

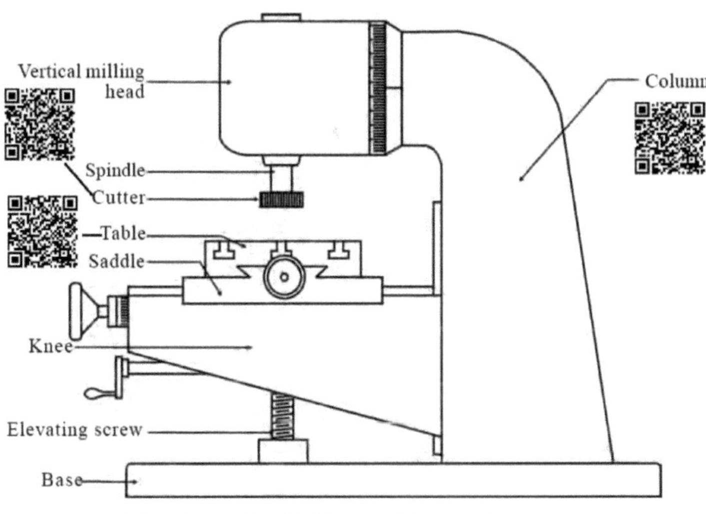

Vertical Milling Machine

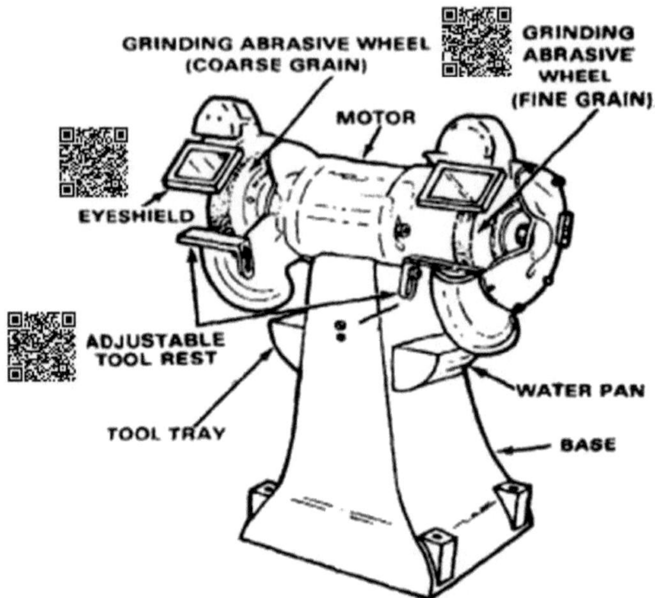

Pedastal Grinding Machine

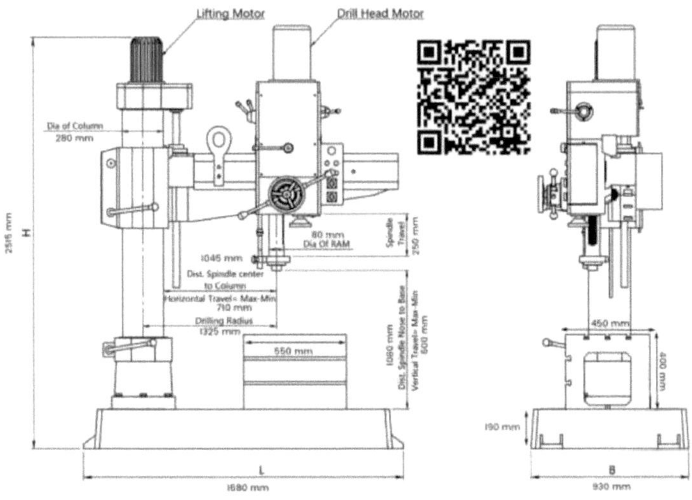

Radial Drilling Machine

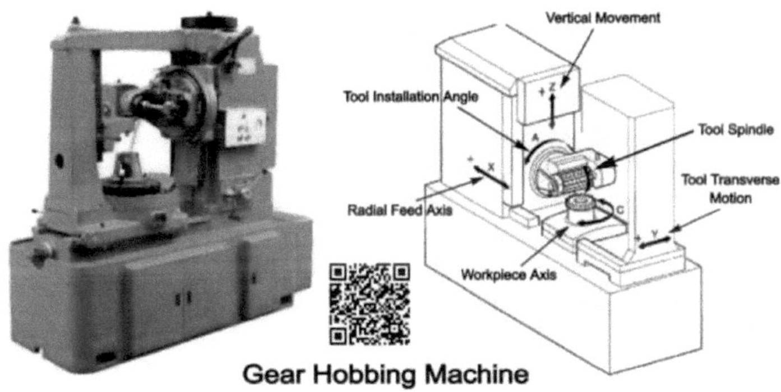

Gear Hobbing Machine

DOUBLE HOUSING PLANER

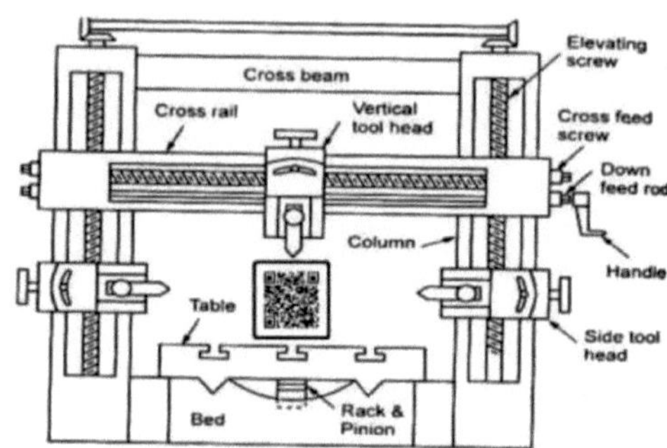

PIT PLANER

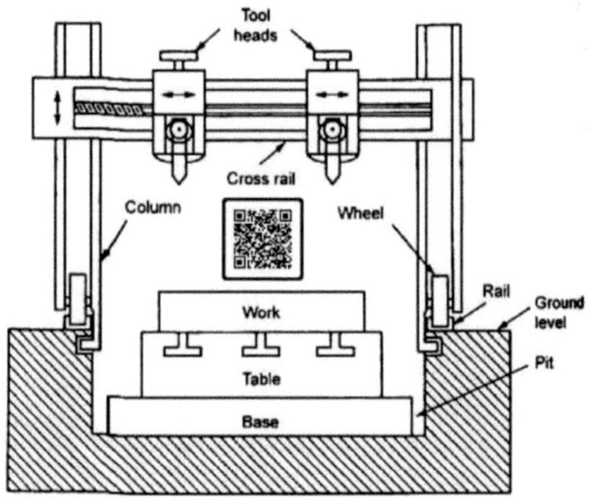

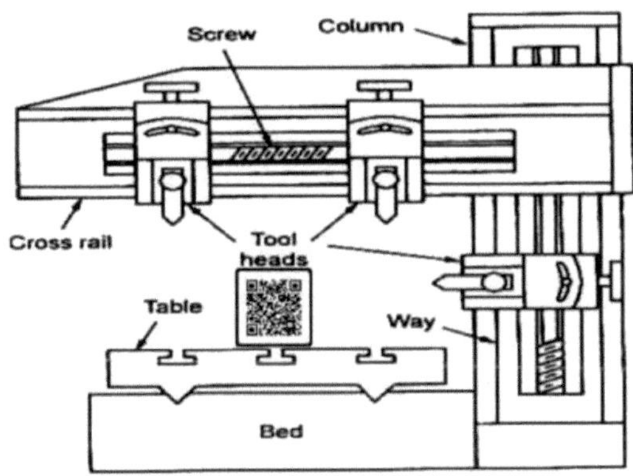

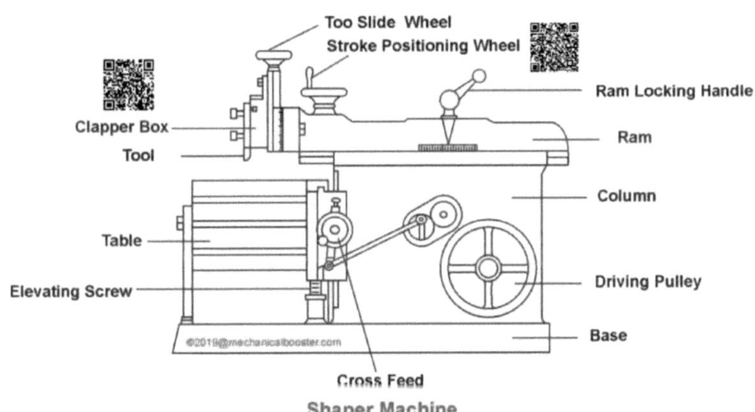

Shaper Machine

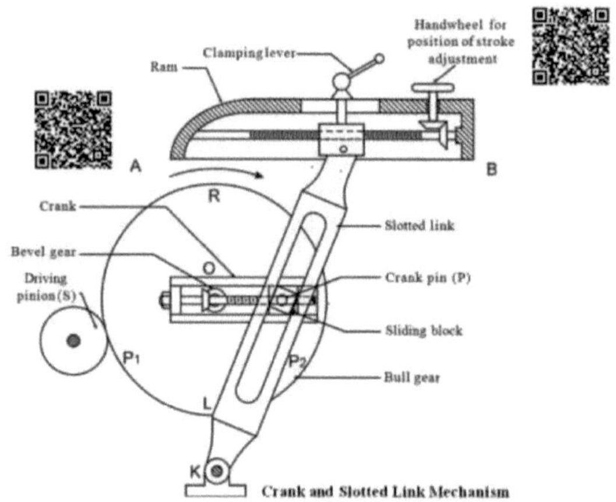

Quick Return Mechanism of Shaper Machine

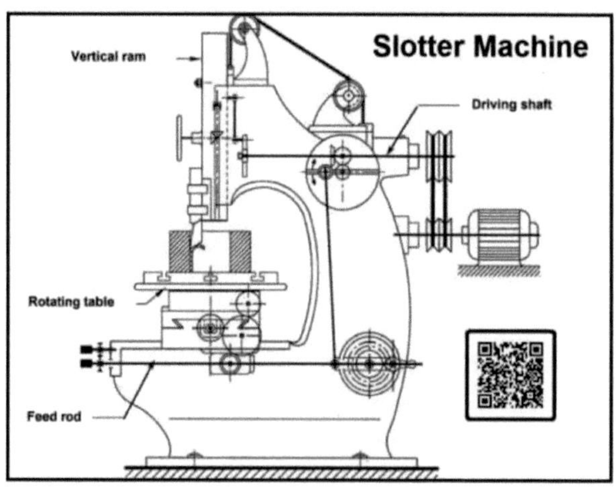

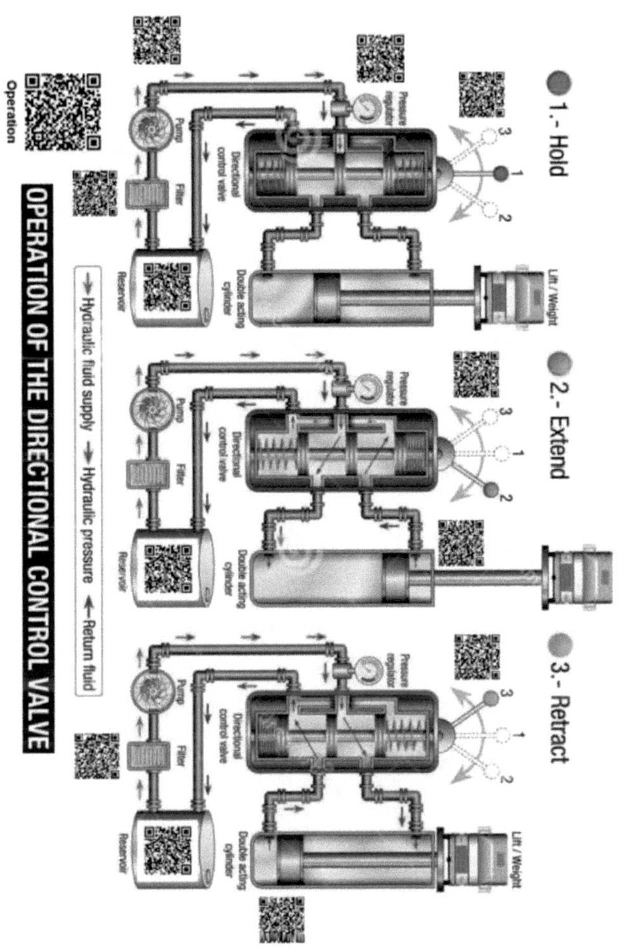
1.- Hold
2.- Extend
3.- Retract
1
2
3
Pressure regulator
Directional control valve
Pump
Filter
Reservoir
Double acting cylinder
Lift / Weight
Hydraulic fluid supply
Hydraulic pressure
Return fluid
OPERATION OF THE DIRECTIONAL CONTROL VALVE
Operation

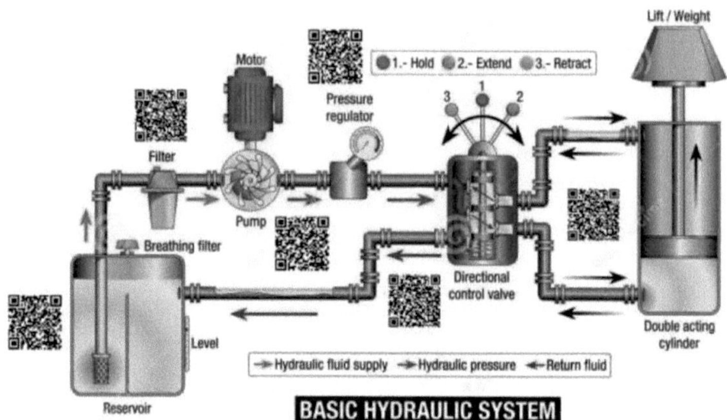

Direct Pressure Relief Valves

- The pressure relief valve provides protection against overload experienced by the actuators in a hydraulic system. One important function is to limit the force or torque produced by the hydraulic cylinders or motors.

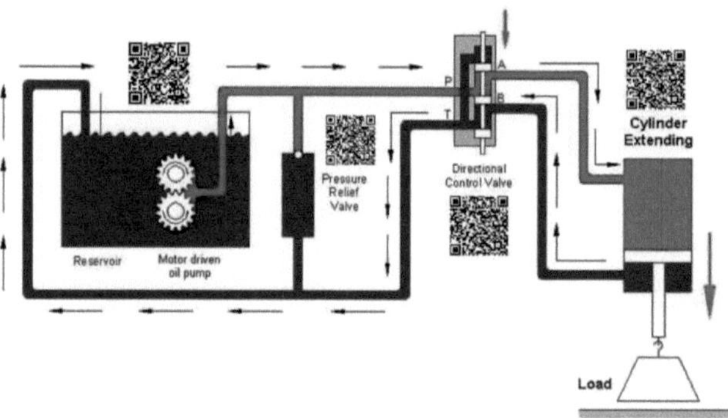

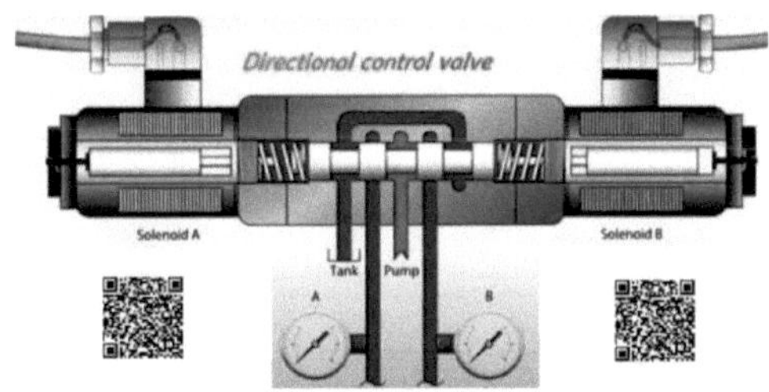

Double Acting, Single ended Cylinder

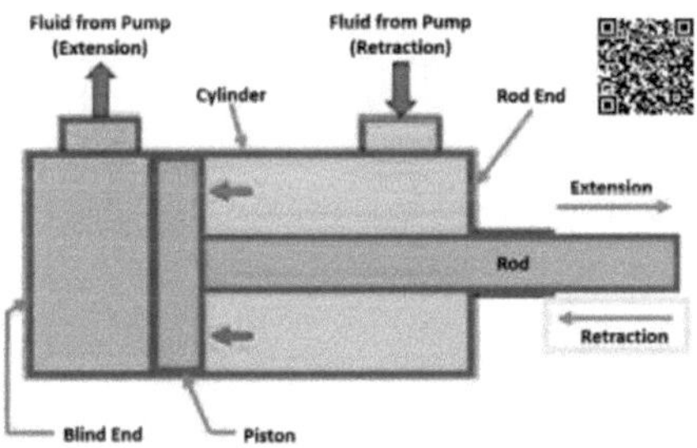

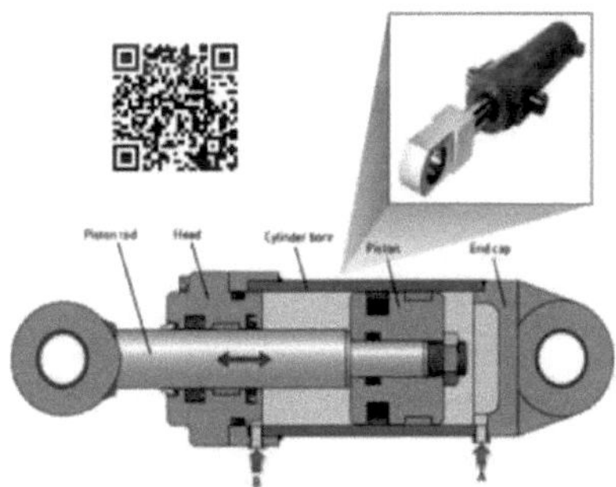

Hydraulic Cylinder

FLOW CONTROL VALVES

- A flow control valve can regulate the flow or pressure of the fluid.
- The fluid flow is controlled by varying area of the valve opening through which fluid passes.

GLOBE VALVE BUTTERFLY VALVE

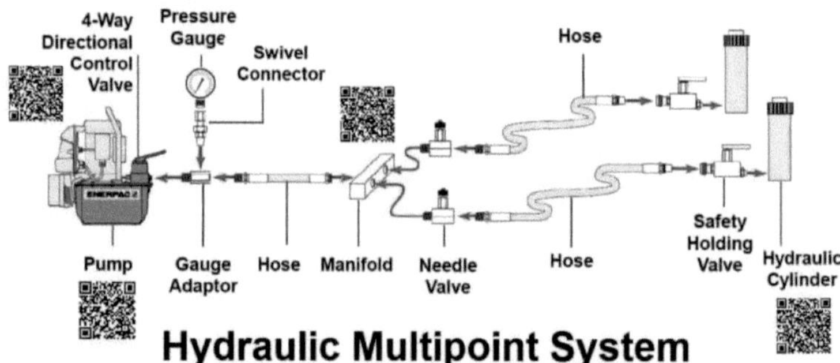

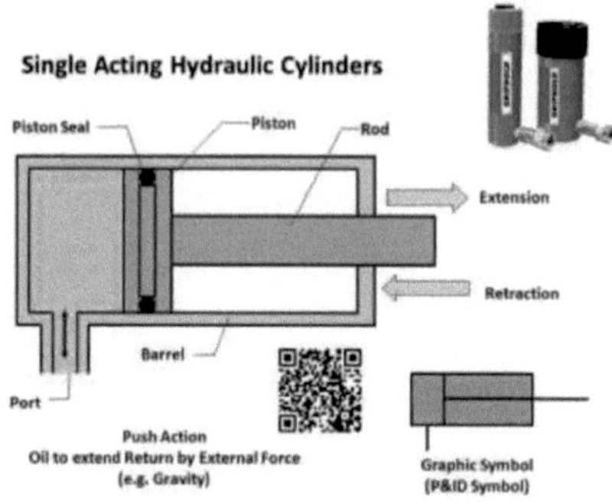

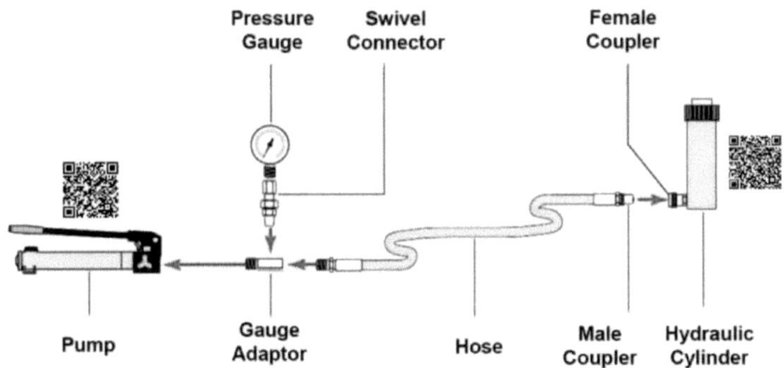

Hydraulic Single Point System

Types of Hydraulic Valves

- **Directional Control Valve:**

  Control the direction of flow of the hydraulic fluid to different lines in the circuit

- **Flow Control Valves:**

  Control the amount of fluid flow in the circuit

- **Pressure Control Valves:**

  Control the pressure in different segments in the circuit

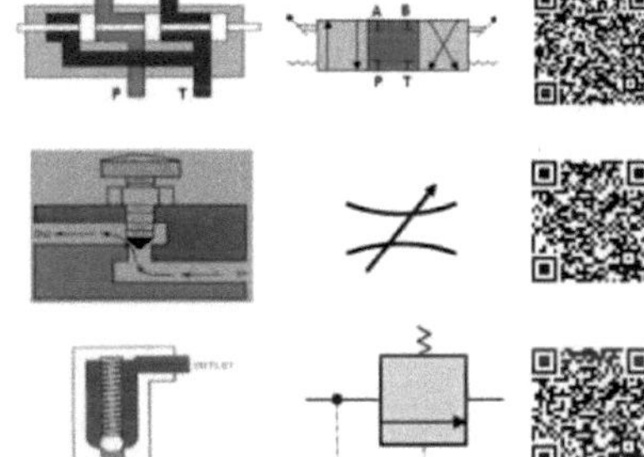

Hydraulic Valves - Parts and Components

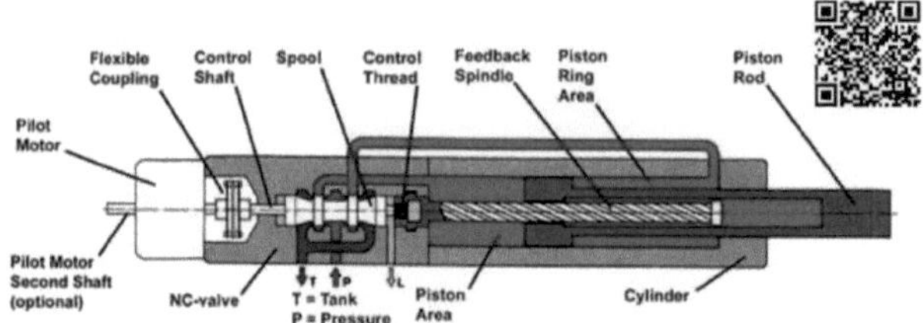

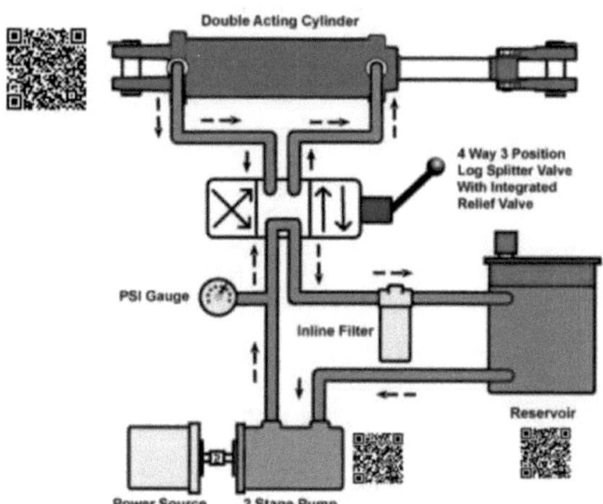

Hydraulic Double Acting Cylinder

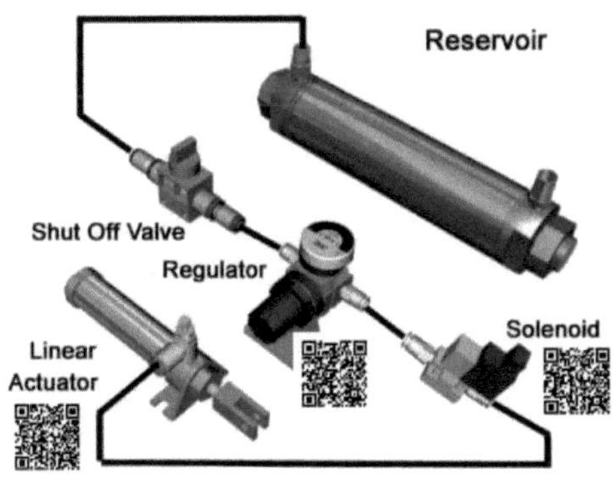

Pneumatic System

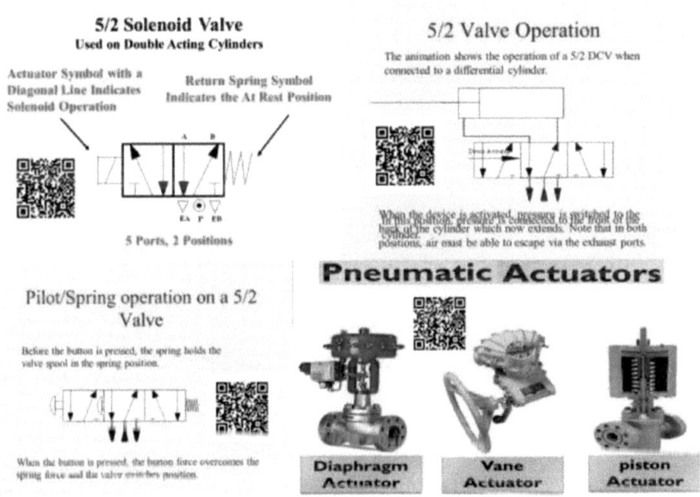

Pneumatic Control Valve

Pneumatic Control Valve Mechanisem

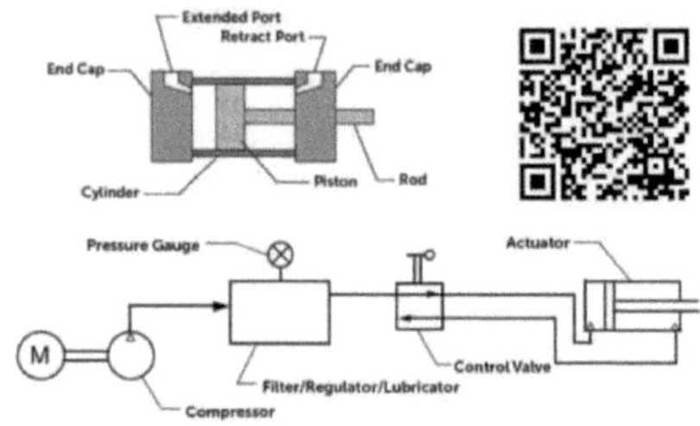

Pneumatic Cylinder System

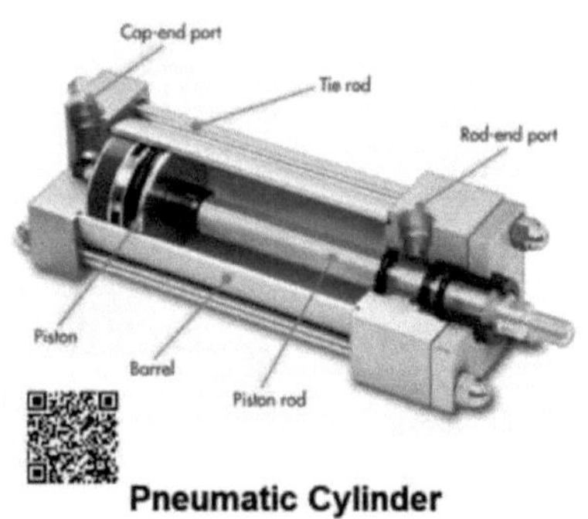

Pneumatic Cylinder

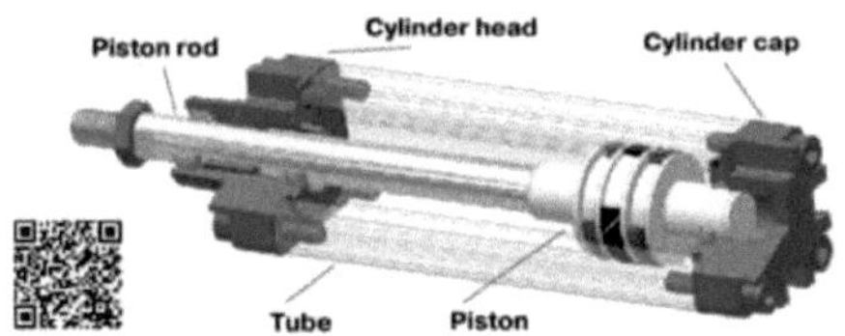

2-way, 2-position, normally closed direct-acting solenoid valve, spring return

4-way (5-port), 2-position, piloted solenoid valve, spring return

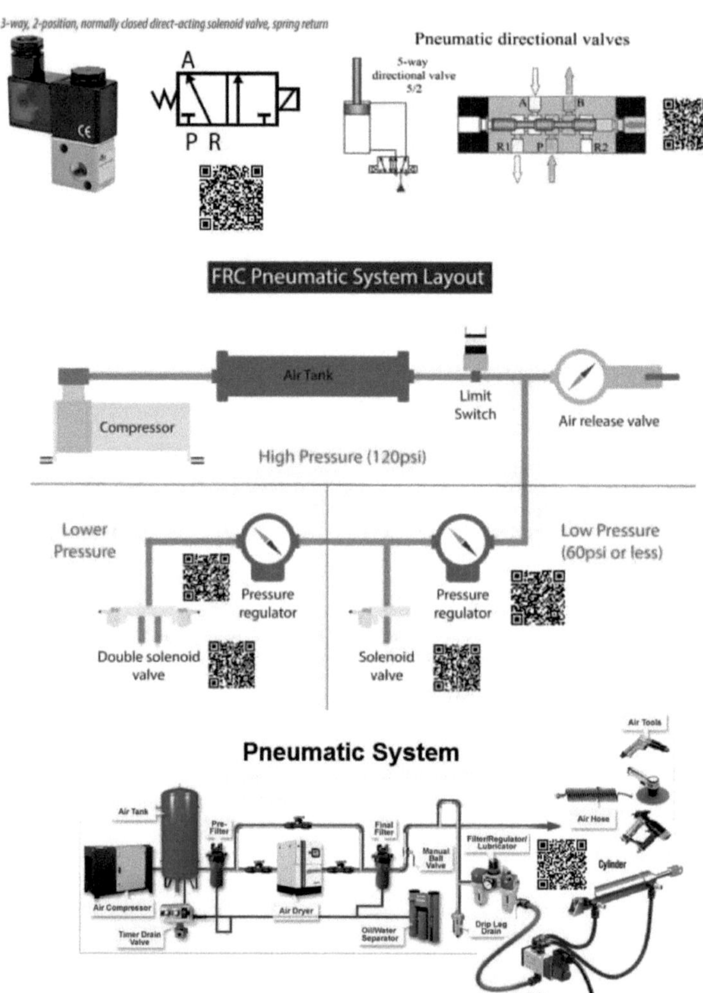
3-way, 2-position, normally closed direct-acting solenoid valve, spring return
A
P R
Pneumatic directional valves
5-way
directional valve
5/2
A
B
R1
P
R2
FRC Pneumatic System Layout
Air Tank
Limit
Switch
Air release valve
Compressor
High Pressure (120psi)
Lower
Pressure
Pressure
regulator
Pressure
regulator
Low Pressure
(60psi or less)
Double solenoid
valve
Solenoid
valve
Pneumatic System
Air Tools
Air Tank
Pre-
Filter
Final
Filter
Air Hose
Manual
Ball
Valve
Filter/Regulator/
Lubricator
Cylinder
Air Compressor
Air Dryer
Timer Drain
Valve
Oil/Water
Separator
Drip Leg
Drain
Valve

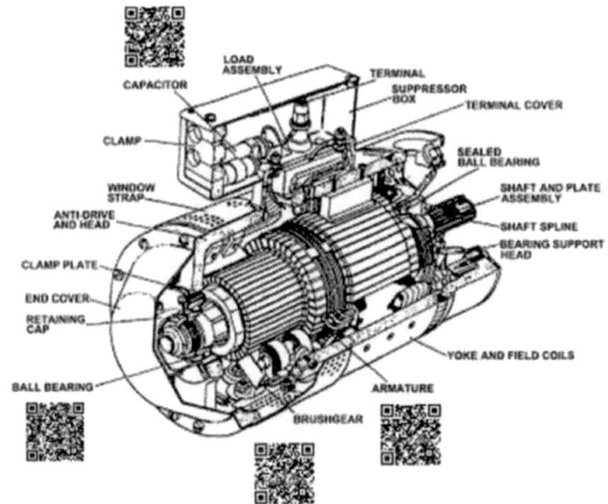

Electrical Generator

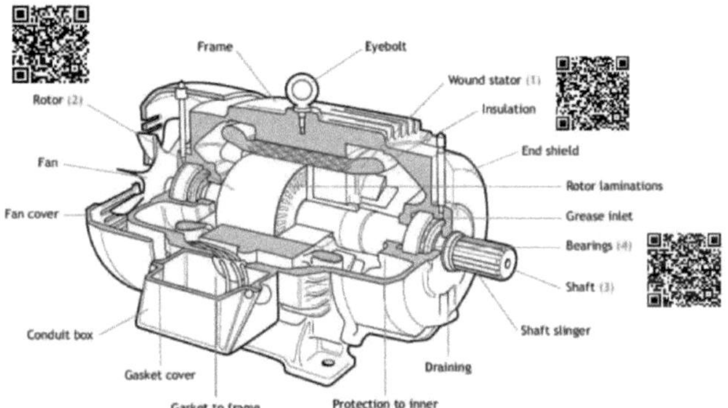

Electrical Induction Motor

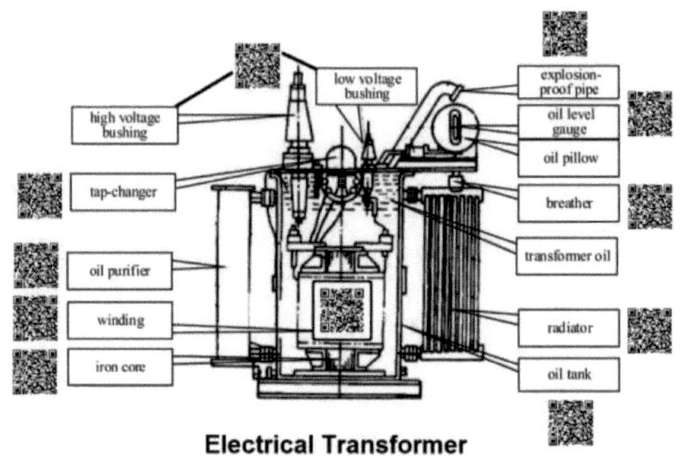

Electrical Transformer

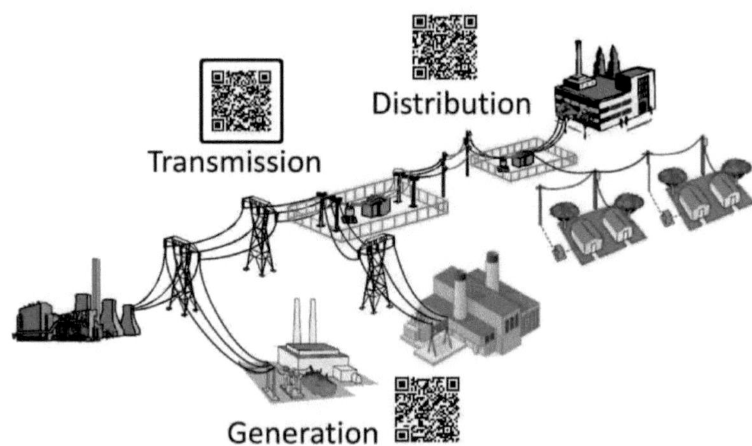

Electrical Power Distribution

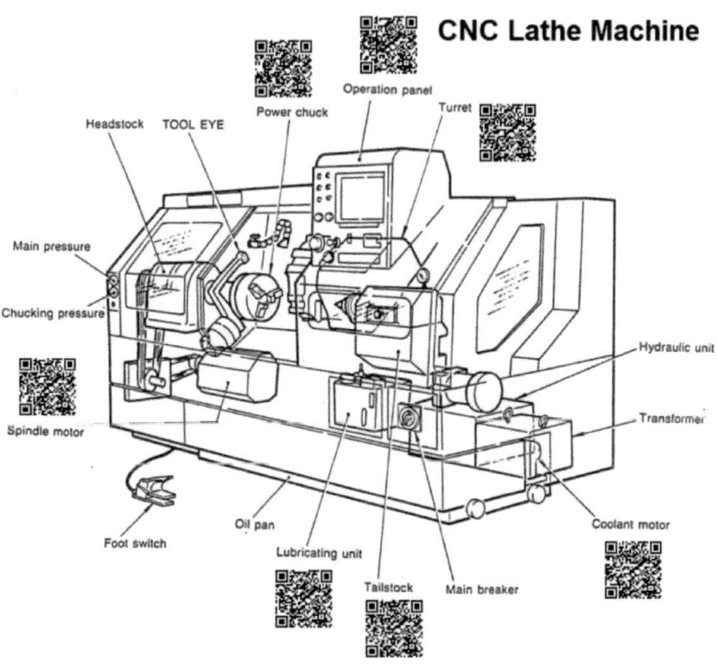
CNC Lathe Machine
Operation panel
Power chuck
Turret
Headstock
TOOL EYE
Main pressure
Chucking pressure
Hydraulic unit
Transformer
Spindle motor
Oil pan
Foot switch
Lubricating unit
Coolant motor
Tailstock
Main breaker

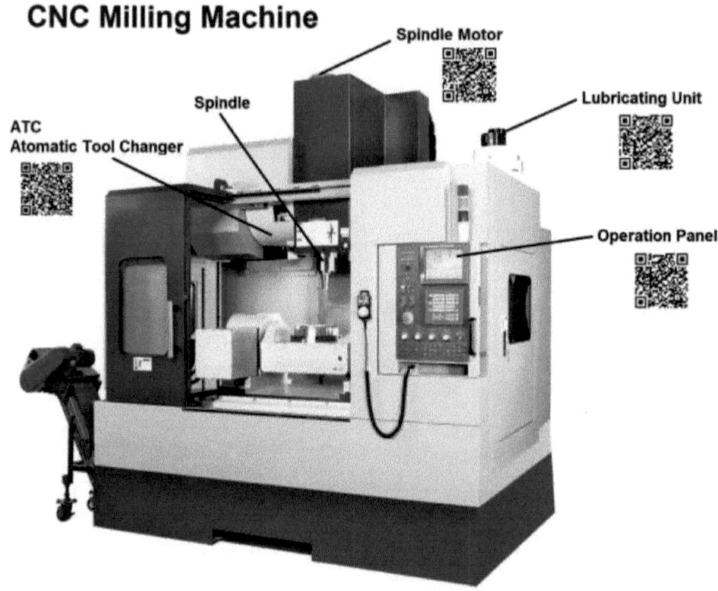

CNC Machine Lubrication

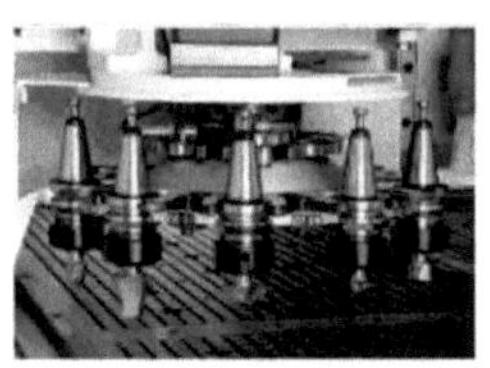

ATC Automatic Tool Changer

Animation & Video

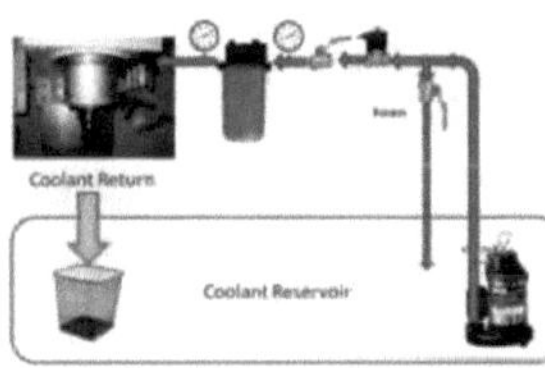

CNC Coolant Pump

Animation & Video

CHAPTER TWO

Mechanic Machine Tool Maintenance Second Year MCQ

1] The cutting angle for a straight snip is...

A] 60°

B] 70°

C] 82°

D] 87°

2] Which method of development is used for developing a rectangular tray?

A] triangular method

B] radial line method

C] parallel line method

D] trial and error method

3] What is the profile of the knife cutting edge of the upper blade of the hand level shear?

A] curved

B] straight

C] inclined

D] beveled

4] For what purpose a groover is used in sheet metal work?

A] to make a hem

B] to make grooves

C] to close and lock the seams

D] to strength then the edge of a job

5] Which type of stake is to be selected for making sharp bends, folding of edges of sheet metal?

A] hatchet stake

B] beak iron stake

C] square edge stake

D] tinman's anvil stake

6] Ammonium chloride is used as a flux for soldering...

A] steel

B] aluminium

C] galvanized iron

D] stainless steel

7] Name the tool used to make and finish the leak proof joints of a pipe T joint

A] groover

B] setting hammer

C] creasing hammer

D] round bottom stake

Hammer Animation Videos

8] Which one of the following metals will not permit X-rays to pass through?

A] stainless steel

B] aluminium

C] lead

D] tin

9] The frequency of up and down vibration of the cutting edge in a nibbling machine is...

A] 1000 to 1500 times

B] 1500 to 2500 times

C] 2800 to 3000 times

D] 3000 to 3500 times

10] Name the instrument used to check the perpendicularity of the branch pipe with the main pipe of a pipe T joint

A] protractor

B] try square

C] spirit level

D] straight edge

11] Which type of notch is used when a single hem meets at right angles?

A] V notch

B] slit notch

C] slant notch

D] square notch

12] To cut out small apertures which punch and die type of machine is used?

A] shear type nibbler

B] punch type nibbler

C] circular cutting machine

D] guillotine shearing machine

13] The overheating of the blow pipe nozzle is to be avoided because it will

A] cause back fire

B] consume more oxygen and acetylene

C] create burn through defect in the joint

D] create undercut defect in the joint

14] State the nozzle size you will select to weld a 3.15mm thick mild steel sheet

A] 3

B]5

C] 7

D] 10

15] The type of flame to be set for welding brass is...

A] air acetylene flame

B] neutral flame

C] oxidizing flame

D] carburizing flame

16] What is the maximum thickness of mild steel sheet recommended for gas welding using leftward technique?

A] 12mm
B] 10mm
C] 8mm
D] 5mm

17]The distance between the root and toe of a fillet weld is called...

A] root gap
B] leg length
C] reinforcement
D] throat thickness

18] Name the weld defect which occurs due to improper cleaning of the mild steel sheet edge and surface

A] lack of root penetration
B] burn through
C] undercut
D] porosity

19] Which of the following mechanical properties of metals gives resistance to pulling forces?

A] toughness
B] ductility
C] hardness
D] tensile strength

20] The angle of below pipe to the line of weld in leftward welding technique is...

A] 40 to 50°
B] 50 to 60°
C] 60 to 70°
D] 70 to 80°

21] The pressure of acetylene gas for gas cutting a 10mm M.S plate is...

A] 0.15 kgf/cm2
B] 0.5 kgf/cm2
C] 1.0 kgf/cm2
D] 1.5 kgf/cm2

22] What size of the cutting nozzle you will select for cutting 10mm thick mild steel?

A] 0.8 mm
B] 1.2 mm
C] 1.6 mm

D] 2.0 mm

23] The angle of filler rod in case of rightward welding technique is...

A] 10 to 20◦

B] 20 to 30◦

C] 30 to 40◦

D] 40 to 50◦

24] One of the advantages of the high pressure system of gas welding is...

A] it is cheaper

B] it is portable

C] it is less dangerous

D] it does not require a skilled welder

25] Soldering of M.S sheets takes place at a temperature of...

A] 150◦C

B] 250◦C

C] 400◦C

D] 850◦C

26] Forge welding is classified as...

A] fusion welding without pressure

B] fusion welding with pressure

C] non-fusion welding without pressure

D] no-fusion welding with pressure

27] The function of a gas regulator is...

A] get different types of flames

B] mix the gases in the required proportion

C] change the volume of gas flowing to the blow pipe

D] set the working pressure

28] For welding a lap fillet joint in vertical position by gas what should be the angle of below pipe to the line of weld?

A] 30◦ to 40◦

B] 45◦to 50◦

C] 60◦ to 70◦

D] 75◦ to 80◦

29] Name the defect, in which the weld metal is flowing on to the surface of the base metal without fusing it

A] crater

B] overlap

C] lack of fusion

D] excessive convexity

30] What should be the angle of blow pipe between the two sheets while welding a T joint on 3.15mm M.S> sheet by gas welding?

A] 30◦

B] 45◦

C] 60◦

D] 80◦

31] Which metal pipe should NOT be used for passing acetylene gas in order to avoid explosions?

A] galvanized iron

B] stainless steel

C] mild steel

D] cooper

32] he percentage of carbon in acetylene gas is...

A] 99%

B] 92.3%

C] 89.1%

D] 85.3%

33] Acetylene gas contains

A] calcium, carbon and hydrogen

B] calcium and hydrogen

C] calcium, carbon, hydrogen and oxygen

D] carbon and hydrogen

34] In an acetylene purifier the sulphureted and phosphorated hydrogen are removed by...

A] pumice

B] water

C] filter wool

D] purifying chemicals

35]A hydraulic back pressure valve is used to...

A] increase the pressure of oxygen gas

B] increase the pressure of acetylene gas

C] prevent the danger of back fire

D] decrease the pressure of oxygen

36] The nozzle size required to weld a M S pipe elbow joint with 3WT to get full depth fusion and good penetration is...

A] 5

B] 7
C] 10
D] 13
37] The selection of nozzle for pipe welding depends upon...
A] groove angle
B] welding position
C] pipe wall thickness
D] diameter of pipe
38] One of the functions of flux in gas welding is...
A] dissolve the metal oxides
B] reduce the melting point of mental
C] increase the flame temperature
D] increase the root penetration
39] The angle of vee groove of a single vee but joint for cast iron welding is...
A] 60°
B] 70°
C] 80°
D] 90°
40] On which of the following factors, the choice of flux for gas welding depend?
A] type of material to be joined
B] type of edge penetration
C] type of fuel gas
D] type of flame used
41.What is the nozzle size required to bronze weld 10mm thick cast iron job?
A] 5
B] 7
C] 10
D] 13
42] State the suitable filler rod for bronze welding of cast iron
A] brass
B] silicon bronze
C] manganese bronze
D] super silicon cast iron

43] In bronze welding of cast iron, the base metal is heated upto a temperature of...

A] 300◦C

B] 650◦C

C] 1000◦C

D] 1300◦C

44] Name the filler rod used for fusion welding of copper

A] manganese bronze rod

B] copper silver alloy rod

C] silicon bronze rod

D] pure copper rod

45] The divergence allowance required for gas welding a 300mm long copper butt joint is...

A] 1 to 2 mm

B] 2 to 3 mm

C] 3 to 4 mm

D] 4 to 5 mm

46] The type of edge preparation done for gas welding a 4mm thick copper butt joint is...

A] single bevel

B] single V

C] double V

D] square

47] The nozzle size used for bronze welding of a 3.15 mm thick copper butt joint is...

A] 5

B] 7

C] 10

D] 13

48] State the filler rod size required for welding a butt joint on 3mm thick brass sheet

A] 1.6 mm

B] 2 mm

C] 2.5 mm

D] 3 mm

49] Name the weld defect which will occur if a No] 3 nozzle is used for welding a 3 mm thick brass sheet

A] undercut

B] burn through

C] porosity

D] lack of penetration

50] The size of nozzle used to gas weld 3.15 mm thick aluminium butt joint is...

A] 13

B] 10

C] 7

D] 5

51] Nozzle size used for welding a 2 mm thick stainless steel sheet as a butt joint is...

A] 2

B] 3

C] 5

D] 7

52] What is the value of preheating temperature for gas welding of aluminium?

A] 100 to 120◦C

B] 150 to 180◦C

C] 180 to 200◦C

D] 210 to 250◦C

53] In soldering operation the base metal is...

A] not heated

B] heated to 200◦C

C] heated to 650◦C

D] heated to red hot condition

54] For welding dissimilar metals, the following property of both the metals should not have wide variations

A] ductility

B] tensile strength

C] thermal expansion

D] wear resistance

55] Name the flux used for brazing of M.S] sheets

A] hydrochloric acid

B] zinc chloride

C] tallow resin

D] borax

56] In progressive gouging to what angle the gouging torch angle is reduced from the starting angle of 30◦?

A] 20 to 25◦

B] 15 to 20◦

C] 10 to 15◦

D] 5 to 10◦

57] The thermit mixture used in thermit welding can be ignited with an initial temperature of..

A] 1500◦C

B] 1200◦C

C] 1000◦C

D] 500◦C

58] Shielded metal arc welding is classified under the process of...

A] electric resistance welding

B] special welding

C] electric arc welding

D] electro gas welding

59] How to specify the size of an electrode holder?

A] by its weight

B] by its shape

C] by its current carrying capacity

D] by the metal used for making it

60] The current set for a 3.15mm medium coated mild steel electrode is...

A] 50 to 80 amp

B] 90 to 120 amp

C] 120 to 150 amp

D] 150 to 170 amp

61] Which method of cleaning you will use to remove oil, grease and paint from the surface of the metals to be welded?

A] filing

B] wire brushing

C] washing with cold water

D] using solvents of diluted hydrochloric acid

62] In the electrode coding ER4211, the third digit of the number 4211 indicates....

A] welding current and voltage condition
B] elongation and impact properties
C] tensile strength of the joint
D] welding position

63] A long arc is used in...
A] welding with a low hydrogen electrode
B] horizontal position
C] plug or slot welding
D] cast iron welding

64] If the travel speed of electrode is high, which type of weld defect you will get on a T fillet joint?
A] overlap
B] slag inclusion
C] excessive reinforcement
D] lack of root penetration

65] Which weld defect occurs on a lap fillet joint due to improper weaving of the electrode in the covering/final run?
A] crack
B] undercut
C] lack of fusion
D] edge of plate melted off

66] A lap fillet weld has uneven bead height] What is the cause for this defect?
A] use of high current
B] low welding travel speed
C] use of wrist movement for the electrode weaving
D] high welding travel speed

67] The coating factor used to make medium coated electrode is...
A] 1.25 to 3
B] 1.4 to 1.5
C] 1.6 to 2.2
D] above 2.2

68] Which type of coated electrodes are used for general purpose welding and for training purposes in ITIs?
A] basic coated
B] iron powder
C] cellulosic
D] rutile

69] Maintaining a key hole and use of proper root gap in a single V butt joint will ensure...

A] reducing the arc blow effect

B] faster metal deposition

C] proper root penetration

D] proper reinforcement

70] At what angle the electrode is to be held with the bottom surface of the joint in horizontal position?

A] 60◦ to 70◦

B] 70◦ to 80◦

C] 80◦ to 90◦

D] 90◦ to 100◦

71] Upto which temperature a moisture affected (wet) electrode is to be heated for one hour?

A] 50 to 100◦C

B] 110 to 150◦C

C.160 to 200◦C

D] 200 to 250◦C

72] The purpose of presenting the plate while welding a T fillet joint is to...

A] get good root penetration

B] avoid crater defect

C] control distortion

D] control arc blow

73] Lack of penetration in a butt welded joint is due to...

A] too low welding speed

B] short arc length

C] high current

D] low current

74]Which type of distortion can be controlled by presenting of plates to be welded?

A] angular distortion

B] transverse distortion

C] longitudinal distortion

D] distortion due to locked-up stresses

75] What is the percentage carbon present in mild steel?

A] 0.05 to 0.1%

B] 0.15 to 0.3%

C] 0.5 to 0.8%

D] 0.8 to 1.4%

76] If a high carbon steel plate is heated to above its higher critical temperature and then suddenly cooled, it will become...

A] annealed

B] tempered

C] hardened

D] normalized

77] Residual stresses present in a welded job will

A] increase hardness of the weld

B] decrease ductility of the weld

C] crack the joint when load is applied

D] increase the life of a welded joint

78] Which one of the following metal has highest thermal conductivity?

A] zinc

B] copper

C] mild steel

D] aluminium

79] Which one of the following metal has the highest melting temperature?

A] copper

B] tungsten

C] aluminium

D] mild steel

80] Which one of the below given welding machines can be used for both AC and DC welding?

A] engine driven welding generator

B] motor driven welding generator

C] welding transformer

D] welding rectifier

81] The name of the part in a DC welding generator which converts the AC supply voltage into DC welding output voltage is...

A] armature

B] commutator

C] field coils

D] carbon brushes

82] Which one of the following is the reason for poor fusion of bead with the base metal?

A] electrode travel too slow

B] current too high

C] <u>current too low</u>

D] arc too short

83] Which one of the following defects will occurs if the percentage of phosphorus is more in the base metal?

A] slag inclusion

B] <u>surface crack</u>

C] lack of fusion

D] undercut

84] Which method of test you will use to check a surface crack on a mild steel welded joint at a cheaper cost?

A] X-ray test

B] ultrasonic test

C] <u>visual inspection</u>

D] magnetic particle test

85] Which one of the following defects can be tested found by a Nick Break test on T fillet joint?

A] crater cracks

B] surface cracks

C] <u>lack of root penetration</u>

D] insufficient throat thickness

86] Which one of the following metal plates can NOT be joined by projection welding process?

A] tin plates

B] <u>copper plates</u>

C] mild steel plates

D] stainless steel plates

87] In which position of pipe welding, the pipe is fixed and inclined at 45° to both horizontal and vertical plane?

A] 1G

B] 2G

C] 5G

D] <u>6G</u>

88] The current to be set for welding a pipe butt joint with a 2.5mmØ rutile coated M.S electrode is...

A] 50A to 70A

B] 70A to 80A

C] 80A to 90A

D] 90A to 100A

89] Downhill method of welding of pipe is done while welding

A] a thin walled pipe by rolling

B] a thin walled pipe in fixed position

C] a thick walled pipe by rolling

D] a thick walled pipe in fixed position

90] In which pipe welding position all positional welding is required to be done?

A] 1G (Rolling)

B] 2G

C] 5G

D] 1G (segmental)

91] Which property of cast iron makes it difficult to weld cast iron?

A] high compressive strength

B] hardness and brittleness

C] low melting point

D] low fluidity

92] The type of electrode selected for welding cast iron with mild steel plate is...

A] M.S] electrode

B] bronze electrode

C] low hydrogen electrode

D] stainless steel electrode

93] Name the solution used for cleaning the copper sheets during pickling

A] diluted nitric acid

B] diluted sulphuric acid

C] diluted hydrochloric acid

D] diluted carbon tetra chloride

94] Which type of electrode is used for fusion welding of copper?

A] electrolyte copper

B] copper silicon electrode

C] phosphor bronze electrode

D] deoxidized copper electrode

95] The usual defect which occurs on a weld done by low heat input electrode due to improper cleaning is...

A] undercut

B] porosity

C] overlap

D] crack

96] Columbium based stainless steel electrode is used for welding stainless steel joints] The will prevent...

A] Crack in the joint

B] weld decay

C] distortion

D] spatter

97] Porosity in stainless steel weld is due to the use of...

A] short arc

B] less current

C] damp electrode

D] unstabilised electrode

98] Which one of the following is used in the oxy-arc cutting process?

A] flux coated solid electrode

B] bare wire tubular electrode

C] flux coated tubular electrode

D] bare tungsten arc cutting electrode

99] The electrode holder in a carbon arc cutting equipment is made up of...

A] plain carbon steel

B] galvanized iron

C] aluminium

D] copper

100] Coping unit of copying lathe is work on

A] Mechanical power system

B] Hand power system

C] Hydraulic power system

D] None of them

101] The inner formers of a hydraulic pipe bending machine are able to bend pipes up to a diameter of

A] 40mm

B] 100mm

C] 20mm

D] 75mm

102] Which is not the property of hydraulic fluid used in grinding machine?

A] it must not control or absorb air

B] it must not cause corrosion of the moving parts

C] Should have adequate viscosity

D] it must vaporize at the operating temperature

103] Which one of the following is the advantage of pneumatic system?

A] For low cost layout

B] For increasing the rate of production

C] For better working environment

104] Following which advantage of Pneumatic power system

A] For increase production rate.

B] Less cash for layout

C] Good climate for work

D] Above all

105]The pressure of fluid in hydraulic brake system is governed by

A] boils law

B] Charles law

C] Pascal's law

D] none of the above laws

106] the fluid pressure in master cylinder depends on

A] master cylinder piston area

B] wheel cylinder piston area

C] pipe line dia

D] fluid viscosity

107] Allows fluid both way in and out of cylinder

A] Piston

B] Push Rod

C] Primary cup

D] Check valve

108] Seals the compensating port

A] Piston

B] Push Rod

C] Primary cup

D] Check valve

109] Actuates the piston

A] Piston

B] Push Rod
C] Primary cup
D] Check valve
110] Develops pressure on fluid
A] Piston
B] Push Rod
C] Primary cup
D] Check valve
111] Develops pressure on fuel to go out
A] Valves
B] Coil spring
C] Diaphragm
D] Rocker arm
112] Actuates the diaphragm
A] Valves
B] Coil spring
C] Diaphragm
D] Rocker arm
113] Allow fuel to flow in and out
A] Valves
B] Coil spring
C] Diaphragm
D] Rocker arm
114] An overflow valve is used
A] to send back excess fuel from the fuel filler
B] to supply more fuel to the fuel filter
C] to supply clean fuel
D] to take the leaking fuel]
115] Excessive oil pressure in the lubrication system may be due to
A] less quantity of engine oil in sump
B] incorrect adjustment of relief valve
C] less suction effect on the suction pipe
D] none of the above
116] when oil pressure increases above set limit, oil returns to sump through
A] pressure relief valve
B] by pass valve
C] oil filter

D] oil pump

117] Supplies air to front and rear brake

A] Brake actuator

B] Dual brake valve

C] System protection valve

D] Flick valve

118] Operated for parking the vehicle]

A] Brake actuator

B] Dual brake valve

C] System protection valve

D] Flick valve

119] Exerts spring pressure and applies brake when air pressure in system is less

A] Brake actuator

B] Dual brake valve

C] System protection valve

D] Flick valve

120] Distributes air to various circuits

A] Brake actuator

B] Dual brake valve

C] System protection valve

D] Flick valve

121] Air compressor's driven by

A] To start heavy duty engine

B] Starter motor

C] Hydraulic cranking

D] Electric motor

122] Actuates the piston

A] Piston

B] Push Rod

C] Primary cup

D] Check valve

123] Develops pressure on fluid

A] Piston

B] Push Rod

C] Primary cup

D] Check valve

124] Displacement volume of piston

A] |.H.P.

B] Swept volume

C] Mechanical efficiency

D] Horse power

125] Starting point of piston's downward movement in the cylinder

A] T.D.C.

B] Cycle

C] B.D.C]

D] Ignition

126] Starting point of piston's upward movement in the cylinder

A] T.D.C.

B] Cycle

C] B.D.C]

D] Ignition

127] Prevents blow by

A] Piston

B] Piston pin

C] Connecting rod

D] Piston rings

128] Reciprocates in the cylinder

A] Piston

B] Piston pin

C] Connecting rod

D] Piston rings

129] Connects piston and connecting rod

A] Piston

B] Piston pin

C] Connecting rod

D] Piston rings

130] Oscillates in cylinder

A] Piston

B] Piston pin

C] Connecting rod

D] Piston rings

131] The top and bottom halves of connecting rod are bolted on

A] crankshaft man journal

B] crankpin journal

C] camshaft

D] piston pin boss

132] A hole is drilled between crankshaft main journal and crank pin for

A] balancing of crankshaft

B] reducing crankshaft weight

C] lubricating connecting rod bearings

D] reducing crankshaft vibrations

133] Relieves excess pressure of air from the air tank]

A] Air compressor

B] Unloader valve

C] Safety valve

D] Brake chamber

134] Turns core to magnet

A] Solenoid Switch

B] Actuating wire (when heated)

C] Ballast Resistors

D] Actuating wire (when cooled)

135] What is the angle of pipe thread?

A] 60°

B] 47'/2°

C] 29°

D] 55°]

136] What is the use of pipe thread?

A] transmission

B] maintain pressure

C] airtight connections

D] none of the above]

137] What is the depth of the 2" pipe thread?

A] 0.5"

B] 0.640"

C] 0.335"

D] 0.580"]

138] External Thread provide on Rod or Pipe , by Die and Cutting Tool is called ......

(A] Tapping

(B] Dieing

(C] Threading

(D] Grooving

Tap Die Animation Videos

139] G.I pipes are provided externally with

A] no threads

B] parallel threads

C] tapered threads

D] neither parallel nor tapered threads.

Thread Animation Videos

140] in the pipe assembly, the hemp packing is used

A] for easy engagement

B] to fill the gap between threads

C] to avoid leakage

D] to get tight fitting.

141]The sealing compound shall be applied on the pipe threads

A] before hemp packing

B] after hemp packing

C] before and after temp packing

D] none of the above.

142] Used on finished tubular wrench surfaces to avoid marking]

A Stillson pipe

B] Chain wrench

C] Strap wrench

D] Footprint wrench

143] Used for gripping and turning pipes and round stocks in confined places]

A] Stillson pipe

B] Chain wrench

C] Strap wrench

D] Footprint wrench

144] Used for holding large diameter pipes]

A] Stillson pipe

B] Chain wrench

C] Strap wrench

D] Footprint wrench

145] Used for gripping and turning pipes,tubes and cylindricai rods]

A] Stillson pipe

B] Chain wrench

C] Strap wrench

D] Footprint wrench

146] Secures rope to small pipe or rim.

A] Slip knot

B] Bowline knot

C] Square knot

D] Sheep shank knot]

147] It can be folded and carried to any place] Similar to the quick releasing type pipe vice.

A Portable folding pipe vice

B] Chain pipe vice

C] Pipe vice

D] None of above

148] Used to hold pipes more than 63mm to 200mm diameter.

A] Portable folding pipe vice

B] Chain pipe vice

C] Pipe vice

D] None of above

149] Used for quick holding and locating pipes] Used to hold pipes up to 63mm diameter]

A] Portable folding pipe vice

B] Chain pipe vice

C] Pipe vice
D] None of above
150] Provides deviation of 90°
A] Plug
B] Elbow
C] Bend
D] Reducer 'T' branczh
151] Provides change of direction with a long radius at right angle.
A] Plug
B] Elbow
C] Bend
D] Reducer 'T' branczh
152] Used for closing a line which has an internal thread.
A] Plug
B] Elbow
C] Bend
D] Reducer 'T' branczh
153] Provides deviation of'45°
A] Bend
B] Reducer 'T' branczh
C] Elbow
D] Tee piece
154] Provides outlet at right angles to the run.
A] Bend
B] Reducer 'T' branczh
C] Elbow
D] Tee piece
155] Used where a change in ' pipe diameter is required]
A] Bend
B] Reducer 'T' branczh
C] Elbow
D] Tee piece
156] Selection of a former depends on the
A] outside diameter of the pipe
B] wall thickness of the pipe
C] bore diameter of the pipe
D] all the above.
157] A branch type hand operated pipe bending machine is used to bend

A] P.V.C.pipes

B] onduit pipes

C] G.I.pipes

D] copper pipes.

158] The inner formers of a hydraulic pipe bending machine are able to bend pipes up to a diameter of

A] 40mm

B] 100mm

C] 20mm

D] 75mm

159] The included angle of a pipe thread is

A] 60°

B] 47°

C] 55°

D] 45°

160] G.l.pipes are available in a standard length of

A] 5 metres

B] 18"

C] 6 metres

D] 16 feet.

161] The standard pipe fittings are provided with threads conforming with

A] BA

B] BSW

C] BSP

D] Metric.

162] The external threads on G.l.pipes are out easily

A] by tap sets

B] dies and die stocks

C] centre lathes

D] thread rollers]

163] Water flowing from tap even when firmly closed.

A] Spindle bent.

B] Defective washer.

C] Valve on the spindle loose]

D] Spindle thread worn-out]

164] Tap hard to turn on and off.

A] Spindle bent.

B] Defective washer.

C] Valve on the spindle loose]

D] Spindle thread worn-out]

165] Loud noise in the tap when turned on]

A] Spindle bent.

B] Defective washer.

C] Valve on the spindle loose]

D] Spindle thread worn-out]

166] G.l pipes are provided externally with

A] no threads

B] parallel threads

C] tapered threads

D] neither parallel nor tapered threads.

167] in the pipe assembly, the hemp packing is used

A] for easy engagement

B] to fill the gap between threads

C] to avoid leakage

D] to get tight fitting.

168] The sealing compound shall be applied on the pipe threads

A] before hemp packing

B] after hemp packing

C] before and after temp packing

D] none of the above.

169] The function of the Pedestal grinder includes ---------

A] Sharpening of the cutting tool

B] Rough grinding

C] Both (a] & (b]

D] None of these

170] The type of abrasives used for the two wheels of Pedestal Grinder are-

A] Coarse and Coarse type

B] Fine and fine type

C] Coarse and fine

D] None of these

171] The Operation of shaping of the grinding wheel by dressers?

A] Dressing

B] Truing

C] Clogging

D] glazing

172] Dressing and truing of the grinding wheel are --------

A] Exactly the same operation

<u>B] Clone with the same equment</u>

C] Done only for coarse grinding wheel

D] Only for form grinding

Grinding Animation Videos

173] Grinding wheels made out of---------------- abrasive are most common because of its free and cool cutting action]

<u>A] Aluminium oxide</u>

B] Silicon oxide

C] Ammonium oxide

D] Carbide]

174] Which among the following abrasive is mostly used for cutting off wheels for cutting non metallic materials?

A] Aluminium oxide

<u>B] Silicon carbide</u>

C] Diamond

D] None of above

175] Which abrasive particle is used for grinding tungsten carbide tool insert?

<u>A] Silicon carbide</u>

B] A|203

C] Diamond

D] Corundum

176] Which of the following is the natural abrasive?

A] Aluminium oxide

B] Silicon

C] Boron carbide

D] Corundum

177] Which of the following is the manufactured abrasive?

A] Corundum]

B] Quartz

C] Silicon

D] Emery

178] Which abrasive particle is used for grinding steel fittings?

A] Silicon carbide

B] Aluminium oxide

C] Diamond]

D] boron oxide

179] What kind of abrasive cut of wheel should be used to cut concrete stone and masonry?

A] Silicon

B] Al203

C] Diamond grit

D] Glass

180] Aluminium oxide wheel is used for grinding ------------

A] cast iron

B] Cemented carbide

C] HSS '

D] ceramic

181] The bond of diamond wheel suitable for offhand grinding of the tipped tool is

A] Resinoid

B] Vitrified

C] Shellac

D] Metal

182] Which among the following bonds, is used commonly?

A] Vitrified bond '

B] Rubber bond

C] Shellac bond

D] Silicate bond

183] The symbol conventionally used for resinoid bond is ~~~~~~~~

A] v

B] R f

C] B

D] E

184] In grinding practice the term "grade of wheel" refers to ---------‘

A] Hardness of the abrasive used

B] Strength of the bond of the wheel

C] Finish 0f the Wheel

D] Hardness of the work pieces

185] Which bond is used in cut of wheels?

A] Rubber

B] Vitrified

C] Resirjoid

D] Shellac

186] Hardness of grinding wheel is determine by --------

A] the resistance exerted] by the bond against grinding Stress

B] Hardness of abrasive grains

C] Hardness of bond

D] Ability to penetration

187] When it is required to run a Grinding wheel safely at very high speed, which bond should be used? "

A] Vitrified

B] Shellac

C] Silicate

D] resinoid' and rubber

188] in surface grinding what is the suitable range of grain size of the grinding wheel for general purpose surface grinding?

A] 20 to 36

B] 46 to 60

C] 80 to 120

D] 150 to 300

189] AS per Indian Standard, the grain ’46’comes under the group of «w] -----

A] Coarse

B] Medium

C] Fine

D] Very fine

190] The grit size of the abrasives used in the grinding wheel is usually specified by ----------

A] Hardness number

B] A size of wheel

C] Softness or hardness of the abrasive

D] Mesh number

191] Bench grinder are used for

A] Heavy duty work

B] Heavy and light duty work

C] Light duty work

D] Lather work

192] Bench Grinders are fitted on a

A] Base

B] Table]

C] Wheel guards

D] Conveyor

193] Which one of the following is the most commonly used Precision grinding machincs?

A] Surface grinders

B] Tool cutter grinders

C] Cylindrical grinders

D] All of these

194] Surface grinding machine table slides over the ----------

A] 'T' __ 50:

B] 'v' slot

C] 'U' slot

D] Radial slot

195] The purpose of the surface grinder is to

A] Produce curved surface

B] Produce flat surfaces

C] Produce cylindrical surface

D] Produce uneven surface

196] The cylindrical grinding produced may be

A] plain, cylinder and stepped

B] Plan, tapered and cylinder

C] Cylinder, tapered and stepped

197] Which type of grinding wheel is used on tool and cutter grinder to sharpen the milling cutter?

A] Straight cup wheel

B] Flaring cup wheel

C] Dish wheel

D] Saucer wheel

198] is used on tool and cutter Grinders mainly to sharpen milling cutters and reamers

A] Straight cup

B] Haring cup

C] Dish

D] Recessed both sides

199] When using a diamond wheel for cutter grinding, a wheel speed of 1600/mm is recommended] What should be the depth of cut?

A] 0005-0025mm

B] 0025-004mm

C] 004-005mm

D] 005-005mm

200] Which of the following is precision grinding machine?

A] Pedestal grinding machine

C] Cylindrical surface and Tool & Cutter grinding machine

B] Bench grinding machine

D] Hand grinding machine

201] TOOl and cutter are re-shaped by ------------

A] Surface grinding machine

B] tool and cutter grinding machine

C] Cylindrical grinding machine

D] Rotary grinding machine

202] Name the part of a tool and cutter grinder on which wheel head is being mounted]

A] Base

B] Saddle

C] Column

D] Table

203] The error due to faulty centre holes are eliminated by operation of -------

A] Surface grinder

B] centre-less grinder

C] Tool and cutter grinder

D] Cylindrical grinder

204] In centre less grinding, the work piece rest on -----

A] Centre of the chuck

B] Face plate

C] Rest blade

D] Ali of these

205] Which one of the following is not an advantage of centre grinding?

A] Easier handling of the woe piece during loading and unloading

B] Handling of the longer work pieces

C] Both shaft and brittle work piece could be handled

D] Low grinding speed

206] Straight land surface is cut by tool and cutter grinder with-----------------

A] Plain wheel

B] Cup wheel

C] Conical wheel

D] Disc wheel

207] In grinding irregular, curved, tapered, convex and concave surfaces, the grinder used is ~

A] Cylindrical grinder

B] Internal grinder

C] Surface grinder

D] Tool & Cutter grinder]

208] Which type of grinding machine Is used for sharpening of tool is milling cutters/drills/hobs/broaches?

A] Chucking]

B] Tool and cutter

C] Centre less

D] Bench

209] Which type of grinding machine Is used for sharpening of milling tools?

A] Chucking]

B] Tool and cutter

C] Centre less

D] Bench

210] For re-sharpening of milling cutter in tool and cutter grinder, which one is suitable size grinding wheel?

A] 35 grit size of grinding wheel

B] 46 grit size of grinding wheel

C] 60 grit size of grinding wheel

D] 80 grit size of grinding wheel

85] A heater draws a current of 8A when connected to a 240V source] What is the resistance value of the heater element in ohms?

A] 40

B] 20

C] 30

D] 60

86] An electric soldering iron with an 80 ohms heating element is plugged into a 240V outlet] How much current will be drawn by the iron?

A] 2A

B] 3A

C] 4A

D] 5A

87] The alternator in a car delivers 4A and has a load of 3 ohms connected across its terminals] Find the voltage of the circuit

A] 18V

B] 24V

C] 12V

D] 16V

88] Three resistors of 1K ohms, 2K ohms and 7K ohms are connected in series with a 30 V supply] If 2 K ohms and 7 K ohms resistors are open circuited, a voltmeter connected across the 7K ohms resistor will indicate...

A] 10 k ohms, 3A

B] 10 k ohms, 300mA

C] 10 k ohms, 3 mA

D] 5 k ohms, 6 mA

89] A voltage source produces an IR drop of 40V across a 20 ohms resistance, 60V across a 30 ohms resistance and 180V across a 90 ohms resistance all in series] How much is the applied voltage?

A] 180 V

B] 240 V

C] 100 V

D] 280 V

90] Three resistors 27 ohms, 47 ohms and 68 ohms are connected in parallel] What is the otal resistance?

A] <u>less than 27 ohms</u>

B] greater than 68 ohms

C] between 27 and 47 ohms

D] sum of all the three resistances

91] One million and one mege ohms resistors are there if connected both in parallel, what would be the combined resistance value?

A] <u>0.5 mega ohm</u>

B] 0.5 milli ohm

C] 0.5 kilo ohm

D] 0.5 ohm

92] A 24 ohms and a 8 ohms resistors in parallel gets a combined resistance of...

A] 6 ohms

B] 12 ohms

C] 3 ohms

D] 32 ohms

93] Resistors of the following values are connected in parallel, 5 ohms, 5 kilo-ohms, 50 kilo-ohms, 5 mega ohms] Their equivalent resistance will be very near to...

A] 4.5 ohms

B] 4500 ohms

C] 45000 ohms

D] 4,500,000 ohms

94] The resistance of given wire is 2 ohms] The resistance of the other wire made of the same material having twice the length and twice the cross sectional area is...

A] 5 ohms

B] 6 ohms

C] 2 ohms

D] 8 ohms

95] If the area of a metal wire of a given length is doubles, its resistance will...

A] be doubled

B] be halved

C] remain the same

D] be four times more

96].Among the following only one is regarded as resistance wire

A] gold

B] silver

C] nichromc

D] copper

97] Arc heating occurs when the air between electrodes of opposite polarity becomes..

A] moistened

B] dry

C] ionized

D] none of the above

98] The meter used to measure the temperature of furnace is...

A] hydrometer

B] pyrometer

C] hygrometer

D] tachometer

99] in the case of electrolyte a rise in temperature causes...

A] decrease in resistance

B] increase in resistance

C] no change in resistance

D] none of the above

100] Heat developed in a conductor is proportional to the...

A] square of the power

B] square of the resistance

C] square of the current

D] square of the time

101] Out of the four metal/alloys given below, one has almost no change in resistance for temperature change...

A] nickel

B] nichrome

C] platinum

D] manganin

102] A material that is slightly repelled by a magnet is called ...

A] magnetic

B] paramagnetic

C] diamagnetic

D] ferromagnetic

103] A material that can be magnetized only very slightly is called...

A] magnetic

B] paramagnetic

C] diamagnetic

D] ferromagnetic

104] Substances that can be magnetized easily and make very strong magnets are called...

A] ferromagnetic

B] diamagnetic

C] paramagnetic

D] permanent magnetic

105] A substance that has a high retentivity can be used for the manufacture of...

A] electromagnets

B] permanent magnets

C] temporary magnets

D] paramagnets

106] A substance that has low retentivity can be used for the manufacture of...

A] electromagnets

B] permanent magnets

C] bar magnets

D] paramagnets

107] The symbol for inductance is...

A] H

B] I

C] L

D] X

108] Tube lamp choke is the best example of...

A] open circuited

B] short circuited

C] grounded

D] connected to the neutral line

109] The initial function of a choke in a tube light circuit is to...

A] limit the starting current

B] induce high voltage

C] heat up the filament

D] limit the current after starting

110] The second function of a choke in a tube light circuit is to...

A] limit the starting current

B] induce high voltage

C] heat up the filament

D] limit the current after starting

111] The periodic time of a wave from is 2ms] Calculate the frequency

A] 50 HZ

B] 5 HZ

C] 500HZ

D] 5 KHZ

112] How big is the peak amplitude of a sine-wave with an effective value of 220 volts?

A] 311 V

B] 380 V

C] 400 V

D] 440 V

113] The peak-to-peak voltage is 99V] how big is the effective value of the sine wave?

A] 70 V

B] 44.5V

C] 49.5 V

D] 35 V

114] A moving coil voltmeter reads 10 V AC] How big is the effective voltage?

A] higher

B] lower

C] the same

D] 10% higher

115] A moving iron ammeter reads 10 A] how big is the peak current of the oscillation?

A] 7.07 A

B] 1.1414A

C] 70.7 A

D] 14.1 A

116] A current of 2 amps flows through a resistance of 10 ohms] The power dissipated in the resistance is equal to...

A] 20 watts

B] 200 watts

C] 40 watts

D] 5 watts

117] If the frequency changes from 50 HZ to 100 HZ keeping voltage constant, the inductive reactance of coil connected to supply...

A] remains same

B] become half

C] become doubled

D] become 4 times

118] Capacitance is not affected by...

A] plate area

B] distance between plates

C] dialectic material

D] frequency

119] The capacitive reactance of a capacitor varies...

A] directly with frequency

B] inversely with frequency

C] directly with applied voltage

D] inversely with applied voltage

120] A capacitor acquired 3 coulombs of charge when 6 volts are applied across it] It has a capacitance of ...

A] 0.5 farad

B] 3 farads

C] 3 farads

D] 18 farads

121] A capacitor is connected across a 200 volt AC line, its minimum voltage rating should be...

A] 100 volts

B] 200 Volts

C] 300 volts

D] 400 volts

122] when testing a capacitor with an ohmmeter, the meter indicates some resistance] The capacitor under test is...

A] leaky

B] open

C] good

D] short

123] The total capacitance of a 40 micro farad capacitor connected in series with an 80 micro farad capacitor is...

A] 26.7 micro farad

B] 40 micro farad

C] 60.6 micro farad

D] 120 micro farad

124] For obtaining 1 micro farad capacitor from 3 nos] of 3 micro farad capacitors we have to connect...

A] all in parallel

B] all in series

C] 2 series and one in parallel

D] none of the above

125] In an AC series circuit having R and C the current flowing through the capacitor will be...

A] lagging the voltage

B] leading the voltage

C] in phase with the voltage

D] none of the above

126] If the frequency of the supply is increased in the R-C series circuit the capacitive reactance will be

A] reduced

B] increased

C] having no effect

D] none of the above

127] Power companies are interested in improving the power factor to

A] reduce line current

B] increase motor efficiency

C] increase volt-amperes

D] decrease power

128] A capacitor increases the power factor value of an AC motor load when it is connected...

A] in series with the motor

B] in series with the starter

C] in parallel with the motor

D] in series with the main winding

129] Normally, the power factor of an incandescent lighting circuit is..

A] 0

B] 0.5

C] 0.707

D] 1.0

130] When resistance alone is used to determine current in an RLC series circuit, the circuit is...

A] an inductive circuit

B] a capacitive circuit

C] a combination circuit

D] a resonant circuit

131] Inductive reactance is directly related to..

A] resistance

B] frequency

C] capacitance

D] power

132] Synchronous motor when used for power factor improvement should be...

A] under excited
B] over excited
C] loaded
D] running at no load
133] In a RL parallel circuit, the opposition to total current is called...
A] reactance
B] resistance
C] a vector sum
D] impedance
134] In a AC parallel RL circuit, the power dissipated at the
A] impedance
B] resistance
C] inductance
D] capacitance
135] How much is the nominal output voltage of a carbon zinc cell?
A] 12V
B] 1.5V
C] 2.0V
D] 2.2V
136] Cells are connected in series to..
A] increase the output voltage
B] decreases the output voltage
C] decrease the internal resistance
D] increase the current capacity
54137connected in
A] series
B] parallel
C] series-parallel
D] parallel-series
138] The capacity of a cell is measured in
A] watt-hour
B] watts
C] amperes
D] ampere-hour
139] The primary cell which has the shortest shelf life is
A] carbon – zinc
B] alkaline
C] mercury

D] lithium

140] The cell which has very high energy density for given weight or volume to

A] carbon-zinc

B] alkaline

C] mercury

D] lithium

141] A 100-Ah capacity battery should deliver a current of 8A for approximately...

A] 12 h

B] 8 h

C] 20 h

D] 100 h

142] When the battery is needed to be kept idle for a long time...

A] overcharge the battery

B] remove electrolyte

C] clean the plates with distilled water

D] dry them and store the battery in cool dry clean place

143] The active materials of the nickel iron cell are...

A] nickel hydroxide

B] powdered iron and its oxide

C] 21% solution of caustic potash

D] all the above materials

144] The capacity of a cell is measured in

A] watt hour

B] watts

C] amperes

D] ampere-hour

145] To charge a secondary cell, the system used is

A] low voltage AC

B] high voltage AC

C] AC

D] DC

146] What is the number of phases in a normal industrial supply system?

A] one

B] three

C] four

D] two

147] In a 3 phase star connected alternator, the coils have a phase difference of...

A] 120◦

B] 240◦

C] 60◦

D] 360◦

148] Delta connection is used no one of the following

A] primary of the transmission line transformer

B] alternator winding

C] secondary of the distribution transformer

D] primary of the distribution transformer

149] Which method can be used to measure the power in a 3-phase unbalanced load system?

A] one wattmeter method

B] tow wattmeter method

C] three wattmeter method

D] three ammeter method

150] Two wattmeters can be used to measure 3-hase power in a 3-phase, 3 wire system with...

A] balanced load

B] unbalanced load

C] balanced as well as unbalanced load

D] out of balanced load

151] A single wattmeter can be used to measure power in a 3-phase system only when the load is..

A] balanaced

B] unbalanced

C] balanced as well as unbalanced load

D] constant

152] The force producing movement of the pointer in an indicating instrument is called as...

A] deflecting force

B] controlling force

C] damping force

D] distracting force

153] A permanent magnet moving coil instrument will read...

A] only AC quantities

B] only DC quantities

C] both AC and DC quantities

D] pulsating quantities

154] An instrument using gravity control will read correctly if used in..

A] vertical position only

B] horizontal position only

C] inclined position only

D] any position

155] Which one of the following damping methods is used in permanent magnet moving coil instrument?

A] air damping

B] fluid damping

C] spring damping

D] eddy current damping

156] Moving coil instrument works on the effect of...

A] chemical effect

B] heating effect

C] electrostatic effect

D] electromagnetic effect

157] The meter installed at your house to measure electrical energy is an example of...

A] indication type instrument

B] recording type instrument

C] indicating as well as recording type instrument

D] integrating type instrument

158].Which of the following material is preferred for permanent magnet?

A] alnico

B] y-alloy

C] silicon steel

D] wrought iron

159] The instrument which could be classified as absolute instrument is...

A] milli ammeter

B] micro ammeter

C] galvanometer

D] tangent galvanomer

160] Which of the following methods of damping is commonly used in moving iron instrument?

A] Air damping
B] fluid damping
C] eddy current damping
D] viscosity damping

161] The deflecting torque of a moving iron instrument is directly proportional to the..

A] current
B] square of the current
C] square root of the current
D] voltage

162]Which of the following is used for measuring the medium resistance directly?

A] ammeter
B] megger
C] ohmmeter
D] voltmeter

163] An ohmmeter is used for measuring the...

A] insulation resistance
B] resistance
C] current
D] potential difference

164] Which of the following components is not a part of an ohmmeter?

A] fixed resistor
B] variable resistor
C] capacitor
D] battery

165] In shunt ohmmeter, maximum deflection signifies ..

A] maximum resistance
B] minimum resistance
C] a fault in the megger
D] none of these

166].An unknown DC voltage is to be measured, which measuring range will you select first?

A] 500V
B] 50V
C] 1.5 V
D] 0.5V

167].An unknown direct current of micro ampere rating is to be measured, which measuring range will you select first?

A] 20 micro amp

B] 15 micro amp

C] 150 micro amp

D] 500 micro amp

168] A multimeter cannot measure...

A] current

B] potential difference

C] capacitance

D] resistance

169] Dynamometer type meters are used to measure...

A] only AC quantities

B] only DC quantities

C] both AC and DC

D] pulsating AC only

170] Which effect is used in wattmeter?

A] electrodynamic effect

B] thermal effect

C] chemical effect

D] electrostatic effect

171] Which of the instrument listed below operates efficiently as wattmeter in both AC and DC?

A] PMMC instrument

B] dynamometer instrument

C] hot wire instrument

D] MI instrument

172] Electrodynamic type of instrument are used commonly for the measurement of...

A] voltage

B] current

C] resistance D]

173] When the phase and neutral of the energy meter are interchanged, its disc...

A] rotates in reverse direction

B] rotates in correct direction

C] will stop

D] rotates slowly

E] rotates at high speed

174] When the disc of energy meter is rotating even without connecting any load, the error is called

A] creeping error

B] phase error

C] friction error

D] temperature error

175] AC single phase energy meters record the energy in the unit of...

A] kilowatt hours

B] number of thousands of disc rotation

C] volt amperes

D] kilo volt ampere

176] A megger measures resistance in...

A] ohms

B] hundreds of ohms

C] thousands of ohms

D] millions of ohms

177] A megger is exclusively designed for measuring..

A] very high resistance

B] very low resistance

C] ground faults in power lines

D] over loads on DC motors

178] For pipe earthing the minimum internal diameter of galvanized iron of steel pipe required is...

A] 12.5 mm

B] 16mm

C] 3.5 mm

D] 4 m

179] The earth conductor provides a path to ground for..

A] leakage current

B] over current

C] high voltage

D] circuit current

180] if the size of the circuit copper conductor is 10 sq-mm then the size of earth conductor in G.I] wire should be...

A] 1.5 sq.mm

B] 2.5 sq.mm

C] 5 sq.mm

D] 10 sq.mm

181] One calory is equal to,,,

A] 4187 joules

B] 418.7 joules

C] 41.87 joules

D] 4.187 joules

182] The operating temperature range of electrical stove with bare heating element is...

A] 300◦ to 400◦C

B] 500◦ to 600◦C

C] 550◦ to 900◦C

D] 1100◦ to 1300◦C

183] Which appliance works on heating effect of electric current?

A] incandescent lamp

B] bimetallic thermostat

C] H R C fuse

D] toaster

184] What is the size of nichrome wire for heating element of 1000 watts, 230V heater at 500◦C?

A] 18 SWG

B] 20SWG

C] 24 SWG

D] 25 SWG

185] The heat proof insulating material used for heater base is...

A] mica

B] porcelain

C] asbestos

D] glass wool

186].The temperature regulating component of an automatic electric iron is...

A] heating element

B] thermostat

C] sole plate

D] pressure plate

CNC Machine Tape Punch

image

248] Tape punch having 1 inch in width tape it is made by

A] Paper Mylar

B] Aluminum Mylar

C] Plastic

D] Above all

249] In point two point positioning positioning system........] Is acceptable

A] Open loop control system

B] Closed loop control system

C] Above both

D] None of them

250] In CNC machine having.......

A] Lead screw

B] Ball lead screw

C] Above both

D] None of both

CNC Program Coordinate

image

251] The aim of sub program is........

A] For find coordinates X Y Z.

B] For other small machine.

C] To avoid cutting tool nose tool nose penetration in Jobs surface of high speed.

D] While machining of job in special condition do not use time to time of program block.

252] What is mean by while while xyz co-ordinate point measure zero-measurement

A] Reference mark.

B] Work zero

C] Co-ordinate points

D] Above all

253] CNC machine specified by axis......

A] 2 axis

B] 3 axis

C] 4 axis

D] Above all

CNC Machine Axis

image

254] Xyz axis of CNC machines which point is used for measurements.

A] Work zero point

B] Machine zero point

C] Common zero point

D] Above all

255] Following which point is not useful in CNC machine.

A] various operation done on CNC machine.

B] Less amount for inspection.

C] Hard for setting measure.

D] Machine efficiency is depend upon operators skill.

256] For selection of zero offset before necessary..........

A] cutter is fixed on machine table.

B] The data entered in machine.

C] Job is fixed on machine table.

D] Speed and feed selection necessary before machine operates.

CNC Work Zero Offset Setting.

image

257] In zero offset program indicates........] Code of following

A] X y z

B] X0 y0 z00

C] X10 Y20 Z30

D] G71

258] Work zero is

A] Datum of machine zero on job position.

B] Indicate by X0Y0Z0.

C] Selection of point on job according to program.

D] The end of machining point

259] M command is used for starting operation and complete revolution cycle M03 means.

A] Stop the program.

B] Program completed and reset.

C] Complete the program.

D] Spindle clockwise motion.

CNC Machine Lubrication

image

260] CNC machine is not manually operated it is control by...........
A] Program
B] operation
C] Cam
D] Plug board system
261] In CNC machine M13 means
A] coolant stop
B] coolant on
C] spindle stop
D] coolant on & spindle on
262] The function of power pack in CNC machine.
A] For balancing of lubricants heat.
B] For increasing heat of lubricants.
C] For destroy heat of lubricant.
D] Above all.
CNC Machine Bed.

image

263] The section of CNC machine bed is.....
A] Flat
B] Half round
C] Rectangular
D] Triangular
264] Following which statement is disadvantage of CNC machine.
A] Less inspection charge.
B] Less tooling charge.
C] Increase production rate.
D] High establishment charge.
265] The point to point system is more effective for......
A] Turning
B] Profile milling
C] Grinding
D] Drilling
Tool Setting on NC Machine.

image

266] Tool setting on NC machine on......] unit.
A] Presetting device.
B] Order special device without machine.
C] On n c machine other empty time.
D] When other operation working on machine.

267] For measuring system having built-in coordinates in this system..........] is called zero position.

A] Reference point.

B] Machine zero point.

C] Work zero point

D] Program zero point.

268] Job turning on CNC machine 50 mm dia turn with programs said the trial run 50.1 mm at production time following which Idea used for correct dia making

A] by increase offset of tool 0.1 mm.

B] by increase offset of tool 0.05 mm

C] by decrease offset of tool 0.05 mm

D] by decrease offset of tool 0.1 mm

CNC Copying Lathe Machine.

image

269] For measure zero offset dim dimensions on CNC machine.........mode is set

A] MDI

B] Jog

C] Automatic

D] preset

270] Coping unit of copying lathe is work on

A] Mechanical power system

B] Hand power system

C] Hydraulic power system

D] None of them

271] Following which advantage of Pneumatic power system

A] For increase production rate.

B] Less cash for layout

C] Good climate for work

D] Above all

Principle of CNC Machine Templates.

image

272] For face copying........] Type template is used

A] Rounded

B] Plate type

C] Flat

D] Triangular

273]............] Is Main principle of CNC MACHINE?

A] Indicate all states in numbers

B] More time required for mechanical control on machine.

C] Cutting speed is more than manual control.

D] Production sequence in workshop is stored by block number in machine.

274] For copy of one shaft.......] Type template is used.

A] Rounded

B] Triangular

C] Flats

D] Square

CNC Program Tool Path.

image

275] The symptoms of continuous path is

A] Called counting system.

B] Tool and work piece on co-ordinate Axis for inter related motion.

C] By the setting of cutter feed and speed

D] Above all

276] Misc command M30 means........

A] End of program and reset

B] Program stop

C] Clockwise motion of spindle

D] Complete the programs

277] Following which affect on milling surface while by milling with unsetting spindle vertical milling machine with- longitudinal feed.

A] Convex surface

B] Concave surface

C] Radius cross line

D] Rough surface

CNC Milling Operation]

image

278] While milling by vertical milling machine with 12 mm dia end mill cutter through slot provide on mild steel plate the cutter is sleep and broken for this fault how it is avoid.

A] High speed spindle

B] Low cutting speed

C] Increase of cut depth

D] Less the depth and feed of cutter

279] Having 5 mm pitch of screw and dividing ratio of 40 : 1 what is lead of milling machine

A] 0.25 mm

B] 5 mm

C] 8 mm

D] 200 mm

280] If not use of backlash Eliminator slap cutter used for down milling operation which safety to be observed?

A] Less lead and depth

B] High lead

C] high lead and less depth

D] High lead and high speed

CNC Machine Zero & Feed Rate.

cnc machine zero.PNG

281] Zero offset is the distance between.....] And.........

A] G41 & g42

B] Machine zero & work zero

C] Reference point and tapping mode

D] None of them

282] The feed rate is programmed as mm per minute with G ....] And mm per- Revolution with G.

A] G41 & g42

B] G 43 and G 40

C] G 94 and g95

D] None of them

283] For collection all instructions from.......] In CNC control unit

A] Memory

B] Tape reader

C] Control panel

D] Operator

CNC Drilling Machine.

cnc drilling machine.jpg

284] For control forward and backward of- CNC drilling machine y axis.........

A] Spindle

B] Table

C] Clockwise

D] Column

285] M 01 command means.....

A] For stopping programs

B] End of program and reset

C] Stopping programs condition

D] Clockwise rotation of machine spindle

286] CNC machine is founded by American scientist john person in.......] Year

A] 1950

B] 1952

C] 1955

D] 1957

CNC Control, Input & Memory Unit.

cnc control.jpg

287] Name of unit used to command the CNC machine.

A] Control unit

B] Memory unit

C] Input unit

D] Output unit

288] Name of unit used to processing the data in CNC machine.

A] Memory unit

B] Control unit

C] Input unit

D] Output unit

289] Name of unit used to storing the data in CNC machine.

A] Input unit

B] Control unit

C] Memory unit

D] Output unit

Servo Motor in CNC Machine.

servo motor.jpg

290] Name of unit used to calculation of data in CNC machine.

A] Output unit

B] Arithmetic unit

C] Memory unit

D] Input unit

291] Name of unit used to display result of processing data in CNC machine

A] Arithmetic unit

B] Output unit

C] Memory unit

D] Input unit

292] Servo Motor in CNC machine is used to..............

A] Changing tool on machine spindle

B] Driving machine spindle

C] Fixing job on machine spindle

D] Proving job on spindle

Types of CNC Machine.

types of cnc.jpg

293] One of the below part of CNC machine used to changing tools on spindle.

A] Servo Motor

B] Control panel

C] Automatic tool changer A T C

D] High speed spindle

294] One of the below CNC machine in CNC milling category is.......

A] Chucking centre

B] CNC late

C] Vertical machining centre

D] Surface grinding machine

295] One of the below CNC machine in turning centre or CNC lathe category is.......

A] Vertical machining centre

B] Horizontal machining centre

C] Vertical turning centre

D] Profile grinding machine

Miscellaneous Functions for CNC Machine.

miscellaneous function.jpg

296] One of the below CNC machine in grinding Centre category is.....
A] Universal milling centre
B] Cylindrical grinding machine
C] CNC late
D] Vertical machining centre

Grinding Wheel Animation & Video

297] In CNC Machine programming word M indicates
A] Feed rate
B] Spindle speed
C] Miscellaneous function
D] Tool number

298] In CNC Machine programming preparatory function G00 is for.....
A] Linear interpolation
B] Clockwise circular interpolation
C] Counter clockwise circular interpellation
D] Hold

Preparatory Functions for CNC Machine.

preparatory function.jpg

299] In CNC Machine programming preparatory function G02 is for.....

A] Linear interpolation

B] Clockwise circular interpolation

C] Counter clockwise circular interpellation

D] Hold

300] One of the bellow preparatory function G 00 is used in CNC program for.........

A] Linear interpellation or feed motion in straight line.

B] Clockwise circular interpellation

C] Point to point Positioning or Rapid motion.

D] Counter clockwise circular interpellation

301] One of the bellow preparatory function used in CNC program for 3D interpellation

A] G 05

B] G12

C] G17

D] G18

Threading & Tapping on CNC Machine.

threading & tapping on cnc.jpg

302] One of the bellow preparatory you function used in CNC program for thread cutting constant lead

A] G33

B] G40

C] G53

D] G62

303] One of the bellow preparatory function used in CNC program for tapping operation.

A] G-40

B] G53

C] G62

D] G63

304] One of the below preparatory function used in CNC program for milling operation.

A] G62

B] G63

C] G 78, 79

D] G81

Drilling, Boring & Reaming on CNC Machine

drilling boring & reaming.jpg

305] One of the bellow preparatory function used in CNC program for drilling operation.

A] G 81

B] G 82

C] G 84

D] G 85

306] One of the bellow preparatory function used in CNC program for reaming operation.

A] G 84

B] G 85

C] G 86

D] G 90

307] One of the below preparatory function used in CNC program for boring operation.

A] G 86

B] G 90

C] G 91

D] G 92

CNC Program Sequence Number.

cnc program sequence.png

308] In CNC program which letter is used to indicate the sequence number of the block

A] N

B] G

C] F

D] S

309] In CNC program which letter is used to indicate position of linear axis

A] ABC

B] UVW

C] XYZ

D] IJK

310] One of the below letters used in CNC program for Feed rate

A] S

B] F

C] T

D] M

Tool Change & Spindle Speed in CNC Machine.

tool change i cnc.jpg

ATC Automatic Tool Changer Animation & Video

311] One of the below letters used in CNC program for spindle speed in RPM

A] M

B] T

C] S

D] F

312] In CNC program which letter is used to indicate TOOL function number of tool

A] T

B] S

C] M

D] F

313] In CNC program which miscellaneous function used to program stop

A] M03

B] M00

C] M01

D] M02

CNC Machine Spindle Direction.

cnc machine spindle
direction.png

314] One of the below miscellaneous function used to program optional Stop

A] M 01

B] M 02

C] M 03

D] M 04

315] In CNC program miscellaneous function M02 is used to……

A] Program stop

B] Optional program stop

C] End of program

D] Clockwise spindle on

316] In CNC program miscellaneous function M03 is used to……….

A] Counter clockwise spindle on

B] Clockwise spindle on

C] Spindle off

D] Tool change

Coolant in CNC Machine.

coolant in cnc machine.jpg

CNC Coolant Pump Animation & Video

317] One of the below miscellaneous function used in CNC program for spindle stop.

A] M04

B] M05

C] M06

D] M07

318] In CNC program which miscellaneous function is used for Tools change

A] M06

B] M07

C] M09

D] M10

319] One of the below miscellaneous function used in CNC program for coolant on

A] M08

B] M09

C] M10

D] M11

Clamping the Job on CNC Machine.

clamping the job on cnc.jpg

320] One of the below miscellaneous function in CNC program used for coolant off

A] M11

B] M10

C] M9

D] M15

321] In CNC program which miscellaneous function used for clamping the job on machine table.

A] M09

B] M10

C] M11

D] M15

322] One of the below miscellaneous function in CNC program used for unclamp the job

A] M11

B] M15

C] M30

D] M60

Work piece change in CNC Machine.

workpice change in cnc.jpg

323] In CNC program which miscellaneous function used for change of workpiece

A] M30

B] M60

C] M68

D] M78

324] The machine is.........for zero off-setting on CNC Machine.

A] In MDI Mode

B] In JOG Mode

C] In Automatic Mode

D] In Present Mode

325] The feed rate on NC Machine is indicate by ......code.

A] X

B] Y

C] F

D] Z

CNC Machine Axis Position]

cnc machine axis position.jpg

326] The position of axis is indicate by.......code.

A] X,Y,Z

B] P,Q,R

C] A,B,C

D] M,N,O

327] CNC Drilling Machine is on.......Axis Programmed.

A] Two Axis

B] Three Axis

C] Four Axis

D] Six Axis

328] From......unit collect instruction in control unit of CNC

A] Machine Tool

B] Instruction

C] Magnetic Box

D] Memory

Working Graph of CNC Machine]

working graph of cnc machine.jpg

329] For preparing tape of NC Machine----------code is used.

A] EIA Code

B] ISO Code

C] ASC Code

D] None of them.

330] CNC Machine gives more accurate production than convention machine, But it is more expensive because.

A] It has AC cabin

B] It has dust proof cabin

C] It has strong foundation

D] It has more space

331] CNC Machine is working on graphical base the point on digital line, indicated digital points call..........

A] Graph

B] Input Media

C] Co-Ordinate

D] Original Point

Axis Rotary Motion in CNC Machine]

axis rotary motion in CNC.png

332] On CNC Machine for longitudinal feed has.......axes, cross feed......axis and for vertical feed........axis name given.

A] A,B,C

B] X,Y,Z

C] P,Q,R

D] M,N,O

333] For rotary motion CNC machine axis has.......name given.

A] A,B,C

B] X,Y,Z

C] P,Q,R

D] M,N,O

334] CNC Machine means.......

A] Natural Control Machine

B] Pneumatic control Machine

C] Numerical Control Machine

D] No Command Machine

335] The size of parts made by .....] for provide interchange ability properties]

(A] Measurement System

(B] Trial and Error System

(C] Limit and Tolerance System

(D] None of Them

Limit fit tolerance Animation & Video

336] In Mass Production for Quality Control the Production is Manufacture......

(A] Zero Defects

(B] Try Method]

(C] Trial and Error

(D] In Limit Size

337] Interchange ability is using for.....]

(A] For Maintenance

(B] For Mass Production

(C] For Single Piece Manufacturing

(D] For Trial and Error Method

338] Which one of the following is important factor required to achieve the interchange ability in mass production?]

A] Geometrical accuracy]

B] Standardization

C] Dimensional accuracy

D] Surface finish

339] Interchange ability is normally applied for? _

A] Repairing of parts

B] Mass production

C] Single piece production

D] All of these

340] inspection aims at

A segregation of defective components

B conformance of rejection

C prevention of rejection

D sale quality goods]

341] Who is responsible for quality?

A designer

B inspector

C operator

D ail]

342] A failure cost reporting system is used for

A incentive for operators

B inventory control

C finding weak points in design

D finding weak spots in production]

343] The stops and trips are used to

A minimise delays for measuring and gauging

B minimise delays in setting tools

C reduce the number of tools needed

D reduce the time required to set work]

344] The term surface finish refers to the...

A] Shining of a machined surface

B] Type of coating given on a surface

C] Heat treatment given on a surface

D] Roughness or smoothness of a surface

345] The purpose for which lapping operation are carried out ---

A] To refine surface finish]

B] To improve quality of fit

C] To improve geometrical accuracy,

D] All the above

346] Which one of the following is a cold working process by which improvement of surface finish, dimensional accuracy and work hardening can be affected without removal of metal?

A] Burnishing

B] Honing

C] Lapping _

D] Super finishing

347] In the honing Process, the movement of the spindle is ---' -----------

A] Vertical and reciprocating
B] Reciprocating
C] Vertical
D] Horizontal and reciprocating
348] It is the process carried out by using abrasive stick?
A] Lapping
B] Honing
C] Super finishing ‘
D] Burnishing
180] Fluid power circuits use schematic drawings to:
a) Simplify component function details
b) Make it so only trained persons can understand the functions
c) Make the drawing look impressive
d) Make untrained person to understand
181] A pneumatic symbol is:
a) Different from a hydraulic symbol used for the same function
b) The same as a hydraulic symbol used for the same function
c) Not to be compared to a hydraulic symbol used for the same function
d) None of the mentioned
182] Pneumatic systems usually do not exceed:
a) 1 hp
b) 1 to 2 hp
c) 2 to 3 hp
d) 4 to 5 hp
183] Most hydraulic circuits:
a) Operate from a central hydraulic power unit
b) Use air-over-oil power units
c) Have a dedicated power unit
d) Does not have dedicated power unit
184] Hydraulic and pneumatic circuits:
a) Perform the same way for all functions
b) Perform differently for all functions
c) Perform the same with some exceptions
d) Does not perform all the functions
185] The lubricator in a pneumatic circuit is the:
a) First element in line
b) Second element in line
c) Last element in line

d) Third element in line

186] When comparing first cost of hydraulic systems to pneumatic systems, generally they are:

a) More expensive to purchase

b) Less expensive to purchase

c) Cost is same

d) Cost is not required

187] When comparing operating cost of hydraulic systems to pneumatic systems, generally they are.

a) More expensive to operate

b) Less expensive to operate

c) Cost is same to operate

d) Cost is not required

188] The most common hydraulic fluid is:

a) Mineral oil

b) Synthetic fluid

c) Water

d) Gel

189) Which fluid is used in hydraulic power systems?

a] water

b] oil

c] non-compressible fluid

d] all of the above

190) Pressure of 1 bar is equal to

a] 14]5 psi

b] 145 psi

c] 12]5 psi

d] 145 x 10-6 psi

191) What effect does overloading have on fluid power and electrical systems?

a] electrical components get damaged in electrical systems

b] fluid power system stops working without damaging the components

c] both a] and b]

d] none of the above

192) How is power transmitted in fluid power systems?

a] power is transmitted instantaneously

b] power is transmitted gradually

c] both a] and b]

d] none of the above

193) Generally liquids are non-compressible but when a large pressure of 70 bar is applied, petroleum oil can be compressed up to

a] 0]5% of its original volume

b] 1% of its original volume

c] 5% of its original volume

d] none of the above

194) The resistance offered to the flow of fluid inside a piston develops into

a] pressure

b] force

c] stress

d] all of the above

195) At low pressures, liquids are

a] compressible

b] non-compressible

c] unpredictable

196) In hydraulic systems,

a] the mechanical energy is transferred to the oil and then converted into mechanical energy

b] the electrical energy is transferred to the oil and then converted into mechanical energy

c] the mechanical energy is transferred to the oil and converted into electrical energy

d] none of the above

197) Which of the following is used as a component in hydraulic power unit?

a] pressure gauge

b] filler gauge

c] valve

d] reservoir

198) Rotary motion in a hydraulic power unit is achieved by using

a] hydraulic cylinder

b] pneumatic cylinder

c] both hydraulic and pneumatic cylinder

d] none of the above

199) What is the relation between speed and flow rate for fixed displacement vane pump?

a] flow rate increases with increase in speed of rotor
b] flow rate decreases with increase in speed of rotor
c] flow rate is constant and does not change with change in speed
d] none of the above
200) In fixed displacement vane pump,
a] flow rate decreases with increase in working pressure
b] flow rate increases with increase in working pressure
c] flow rate is constant and does not change with working pressure
d] none of the above
201) Which type of motion is transmitted by hydraulic actuators?
a] linear motion
b] rotary motion
c] both a] and b]
d] none of the above
202) What is the function of electric actuator?
a] converts electrical energy into mechanical torque
b] converts mechanical torque into electrical energy
c] converts mechanical energy into mechanical torque
d] none of the above
203) Which of the following is a hydraulic cylinder based on construction?
a] single acting cylinder
b] double acting cylinder
c] welded design cylinder
d] all of the above
204) Which energy is converted into mechanical energy by the hydraulic cylinders?
a] hydrostatic energy
b] hydrodynamic energy
c] electrical energy
d] none of the above
205) What is the advantage of using a single acting cylinder?
a] high cost and reliable
b] honing inside the inner surface of pump is not required
c] piston seals are not required
d] all of the above
206) What is the function of a flow control valve?
a] flow control valve changes the direction of oil flow

b] flow control valve can adjust the flow rate of hydraulic oil
c] both a] and b]
d] none of the above
207) What does the numbers in 4/2 valve mean?
a] 4 positions and 2 ways
b] 4 ways and 2 positions
c] none of the above
d] 3 ways 2 positions
208) Which type of solenoid has more chances of coil failure?
a] AC solenoid
b] DC solenoid
c] both AC and DC solenoids
d] none of the above
209) Which stage in two stage direction control valve is solenoid operated?
a] main stage direction control valve
b] pilot stage direction control valve
c] both stages in two stage direction control are solenoid operated
d] none of the above
210) Which of the following is a gas charged accumulator?
a] bladder type
b] spring loaded accumulator
c] weighted accumulator
d] all of the above
211) How is pressure of fluid under piston calculated in a weighted accumulator?
a] pressure of fluid = (weight added / piston area)
b] pressure of fluid = (piston area / weight added)
c] pressure of fluid = (weight added / piston force)
d] pressure of fluid = (piston force / weight added)
212) Which of the following gas is used in gas charged accumulator?
a] oxygen
b] nitrogen
c] carbon dioxide
d] all of the above
213) The relation for rapid change in pressure and volume adiabatically is given as
a] p0 v0 = p1 v1 = p2 v2

b] p0 v0 = p1 v1n = p2 v2n

c] p0 v0n = p1 v1n = p2 v2n

d] none of the above

214) Why is the pilot operated check valve used in clamping operation?

a] to reduce leakage in spool valve

b] to avoid decrease in pressure during clamping

c] *both a] and b]*

d] none of the above

215) Which area does the part shown below indicate?

a] rod area

b] full bore area

c] annulus area

d] none of the above

216) Which of the following statements is true?

a] Meter-in feed circuits have speed control in two directions

b] Standard block feed circuits have speed control in two directions

c] Tank line feed control systems have speed control only in one direction

d] all of the above

217) Leakage in rotary chucks can be compensated by

a] flow control valve

b] pilot operated check valve

c] accumulator

d] all of the above

218) Which valve is used to block the accumulator from the system for the purpose of safety?

a] pilot valve

b] needle valve

c] detent valve

d] all of the above

219) Which of the following systems generate more energy when used in industrial applications?

a] hydraulic systems

b] pneumatic systems

c] both systems generate same energy

d] cannot say

220) Which type of compressor requires a reservoir for compressed air and why?

a] rotary compressor to avoid pulsating effect
b] reciprocating compressor to avoid pulsating effect
c] both rotary and reciprocating compressors to avoid pulsating effect
d] none of the above

221) Which of the following factors is/are considered while selecting a compressor?
a] type of oil filter required
b] volumetric efficiency
c] viscosity of the liquids used
d] all of the above

222) Which of the following is a component used in air generation system?
a] pressure switch
b] pressure gauge
c] drier
d] intercooler

223) Where is an intercooler connected in a two stage compressor?
a] intercooler is connected after the two stage compressor
b] intercooler is connected between the two stages of the compressor
c] intercooler is connected before the two stage compressor
d] none of the above

224) Which of the following notations is used to represent a regulator unit?
a] 3]0
b] 0]3
c] 3
d] none of the above

225) Which of the following logic valve is known as shuttle valve?
a] OR gate
b] AND gate
c] NOR gate
d] NAND

226) In pneumatic systems, AND gate is also known as
a] check valve
b] shuttle valve
c] dual pressure valve
d] none of the above

227) What is a pressure sequence valve?

a] it is a combination of adjustable pressure relief valve and directional control valve

b] it is a combination of nonadjustable pressure relief valve and directional control valve

c] it is a combination of adjustable pressure reducing valve and check valve

d] it is a combination of adjustable pressure reducing valve and flow control valve

228) Overlapping of signals in pneumatic systems can be avoided by using

a] rolling lever valve

b] idle roller lever valve

c] both a] and b]

d] none of the above

229) Which of the following statements is true for cascade method which is used to draw a pneumatic circuit?

a] signal processing valves are connected in parallel

b] when the number of signal processing valves are greater than 4, the signals are strong

c] cascade method does not consider the cost factor

d] all of the above

230) What is the part, shown in below diagram of 3/2 valve, called?

a] manually operated valve

b] pilot operated valve

c] pressure electric converter

d] none of the above

231) In which systems, spool of the servo valve is operated by a torque motor?

a] hydromechanical servo systems

b] electrohydraulic servo systems

c] conventional servo valve

d] all of the above

232) What does servo mean in servo valve system?

a] it cannot receive a feedback but the desired output can be obtained

b] it cannot receive a feedback and the desired output cannot be obtained

c] it can receive a feedback and the desired output can be obtained

d] none of the above

233) In conventional valves, which component is used to move the spool?

a] torque motor

b] mechanical servo valve

c] solenoid

d] all of the above

234) What is the advantage of DC solenoid coils?

a] DC solenoid coils have high rush in current

b] DC solenoid coils have constant level of current

c] DC solenoid coils have rating of 220 V DC

d] all of the above

235) Which of the following statements is true for a proportional valve?

a] spool of the proportional valve can travel maximum length

b] digital type of functioning is possible in proportional valve

c] proportional valve requires a separate flow control valve

d] all of the above

236) Which of the following statements is/are false?

a] air is non-compressible

b] less power is developed in fluid power systems than conventional systems

c] mechanical linkages used for load handling purposes have high efficiency

d] all of the above

237) The hydraulic system is

a] less precise than pneumatic system

b] more precise than pneumatic system

c] both hydraulic and pneumatic systems are same on basis of precision

d] none of the above

238) Which energy is used to transmit power in hydrostatic system?

a] pressure energy

b] kinetic energy

c] potential energy

d] all of the above

239) Which system uses kinetic energy to transmit power?

a] hydrostatic system

b] hydrodynamic system

c] pneumatic system

d] none of the above

240) If no load is attached to piston rod, the movement of piston assembly is possible when

a] oil overcomes its self weight

b] oil overcomes friction in the piston rod assembly

c] both a] and b]

d] none of the above

INDUSTRIAL TRAINING INSTITUTE

Monthly Test-1, Marks- 20, Date:- _______________

(Every Question Carry Two Marks)

1-6] Ammonium chloride is used as a flux for soldering...

A] steel

B] aluminium

C] galvanized iron

D] stainless steel

2-7] Name the tool used to make and finish the leak proof joints of a pipe T joint

A] groover

B] setting hammer

C] creasing hammer

D] round bottom stake

3-8] Which one of the following metals will not permit X-rays to pass through?

A] stainless steel

B] aluminium

C] lead

D] tin

4-9] The frequency of up and down vibration of the cutting edge in a nibbling machine is...

A] 1000 to 1500 times

B] 1500 to 2500 times

C] 2800 to 3000 times

D] 3000 to 3500 times

5-10] Name the instrument used to check the perpendicularity of the branch pipe with the main pipe of a pipe T joint

A] protractor

B] try square

C] spirit level

D] straight edge

6-11] Which type of notch is used when a single hem meets at right angles?

A] V notch

B] slit notch

C] slant notch

D] square notch

7-12] To cut out small apertures which punch and die type of machine is used?

A] shear type nibbler

B] punch type nibbler

C] circular cutting machine

D] guillotine shearing machine

8-13] The overheating of the blow pipe nozzle is to be avoided because it will

A] cause back fire

B] consume more oxygen and acetylene

C] create burn through defect in the joint

D] create undercut defect in the joint

9-14] State the nozzle size you will select to weld a 3.15mm thick mild steel sheet

A] 3

B]5

C] 7

D] 10

10-15] The type of flame to be set for welding brass is...

A] air acetylene flame

B] neutral flame

C] oxidizing flame

D] carburizing flame

INDUSTRIAL TRAINING INSTITUTE

Monthly Test-2, Marks- 20, Date:- ______________

(Every Question Carry Two Marks)

1-21] The pressure of acetylene gas for gas cutting a 10mm M.S plate is...

A] 0.15 kgf/cm2

B] 0.5 kgf/cm2

C] 1.0 kgf/cm2

D] 1.5 kgf/cm2

2-22] What size of the cutting nozzle you will select for cutting 10mm thick mild steel?

A] 0.8 mm

B] 1.2 mm

C] 1.6 mm

D] 2.0 mm

3-23] The angle of filler rod in case of rightward welding technique is...

A] 10 to 20?

B] 20 to 30?

C] 30 to 40?

D] 40 to 50?

4-24] One of the advantages of the high pressure system of gas welding is...

A] it is cheaper

B] it is portable

C] it is less dangerous

D] it does not require a skilled welder

5-25] Soldering of M.S sheets takes place at a temperature of...

A] 150?C

B] 250?C

C] 400?C

D] 850?C

6-26] Forge welding is classified as...

A] fusion welding without pressure

B] fusion welding with pressure

C] non-fusion welding without pressure

D] no-fusion welding with pressure

7-27] The function of a gas regulator is...

A] get different types of flames

B] mix the gases in the required proportion

C] change the volume of gas flowing to the blow pipe

D] set the working pressure

8-28] For welding a lap fillet joint in vertical position by gas what should be the angle of below pipe to the line of weld?

A] 30? to 40?

B] 45?to 50?

C] 60? to 70?

D] 75? to 80?

9-29] Name the defect, in which the weld metal is flowing on to the surface of the base metal without fusing it

A] crater

B] overlap

C] lack of fusion

D] excessive convexity

10-30] What should be the angle of blow pipe between the two sheets while welding a T joint on 3.15mm M.S> sheet by gas welding?

A] 30?

B] 45?

C] 60?

D] 80?

INDUSTRIAL TRAINING INSTITUTE

Monthly Test-3, Marks- 20, Date:- _______________

(Every Question Carry Two Marks)

1-36] The nozzle size required to weld a M.S pipe elbow joint with 3WT to get full depth fusion and good penetration is...

A] 5

B] 7

C] 10

D] 13

2-37] The selection of nozzle for pipe welding depends upon...

A] groove angle

B] welding position

C] pipe wall thickness

D] diameter of pipe

3-38] One of the functions of flux in gas welding is...

A] dissolve the metal oxides

B] reduce the melting point of mental

C] increase the flame temperature

D] increase the root penetration

4-39] The angle of vee groove of a single vee but joint for cast iron welding is...

A] 60?

B] 70?

C] 80?

D] 90?

5-40] On which of the following factors, the choice of flux for gas welding depend?

A] type of material to be joined

B] type of edge penetration

C] type of fuel gas

D] type of flame used

6-41.What is the nozzle size required to bronze weld 10mm thick cast iron job?

A] 5

B] 7

C] 10

D] 13

7-42] State the suitable filler rod for bronze welding of cast iron

A] brass

B] silicon bronze

C] manganese bronze

D] super silicon cast iron

8-43] In bronze welding of cast iron, the base metal is heated upto a temperature of...

A] 300?C

B] 650?C

C] 1000?C

D] 1300?C

9-44] Name the filler rod used for fusion welding of copper

A] manganese bronze rod

B] copper silver alloy rod

C] silicon bronze rod

D] pure copper rod

10-45] The divergence allowance required for gas welding a 300mm long copper butt joint is...

A] 1 to 2 mm

B] 2 to 3 mm

C] 3 to 4 mm

D] 4 to 5 mm

INDUSTRIAL TRAINING INSTITUTE

Monthly Test-4, Marks- 20, Date:- ______________

(Every Question Carry Two Marks)

1-51] Nozzle size used for welding a 2 mm thick stainless steel sheet as a butt joint is...

A] 2

B] 3

C] 5

D] 7

2-52] What is the value of preheating temperature for gas welding of aluminium?

A] 100 to 120?C

B] 150 to 180?C

C] 180 to 200?C

D] 210 to 250?C

3-53] In soldering operation the base metal is...

A] not heated

B] heated to 200?C

C] heated to 650?C

D] heated to red hot condition

4-54] For welding dissimilar metals, the following property of both the metals should not have wide variations

A] ductility

B] tensile strength

C] thermal expansion

D] wear resistance

5-55] Name the flux used for brazing of M.S] sheets

A] hydrochloric acid

B] zinc chloride

C] tallow resin

D] borax

6-56] In progressive gouging to what angle the gouging torch angle is reduced from the starting angle of 30??

A] 20 to 25?

B] 15 to 20?

C] 10 to 15?

D] 5 to 10?

7-57] The thermit mixture used in thermit welding can be ignited with an initial temperature of..

A] 1500?C

B] 1200?C

C] 1000?C

D] 500?C

8-58] Shielded metal arc welding is classified under the process of...

A] electric resistance welding

B] special welding

C] electric arc welding

D] electro gas welding

9-59] How to specify the size of an electrode holder?

A] by its weight

B] by its shape

C] by its current carrying capacity

D] by the metal used for making it

10-60] The current set for a 3.15mm medium coated mild steel electrode is...

A] 50 to 80 amp

B] 90 to 120 amp

C] 120 to 150 amp

D] 150 to 170 amp

INDUSTRIAL TRAINING INSTITUTE

Monthly Test-5, Marks- 20, Date:- _______________

(Every Question Carry Two Marks)

1-66] A lap fillet weld has uneven bead height] What is the cause for this defect?

A] use of high current

B] low welding travel speed

C] use of wrist movement for the electrode weaving

D] high welding travel speed

2-67] The coating factor used to make medium coated electrode is...

A] 1.25 to 3

B] 1.4 to 1.5

C] 1.6 to 2.2

D] above 2.2

3-68] Which type of coated electrodes are used for general purpose welding and for training purposes in ITIs?

A] basic coated

B] iron powder

C] cellulosic

D] rutile

4-69] Maintaining a key hole and use of proper root gap in a single V butt joint will ensure...

A] reducing the arc blow effect

B] faster metal deposition

C] proper root penetration

D] proper reinforcement

5-70] At what angle the electrode is to be held with the bottom surface of the joint in horizontal position?

A] 60? to 70?

B] 70? to 80?

C] 80? to 90?

D] 90? to 100?

6-71] Upto which temperature a moisture affected (wet) electrode is to be heated for one hour?

A] 50 to 100?C

B] 110 to 150?C

C.160 to 200?C

D] 200 to 250?C

7-72] The purpose of presenting the plate while welding a T fillet joint is to...

A] get good root penetration

B] avoid crater defect

C] control distortion

D] control arc blow

8-73] Lack of penetration in a butt welded joint is due to...

A] too low welding speed

B] short arc length

C] high current

D] low current

9-74]Which type of distortion can be controlled by presenting of plates to be welded?

A] angular distortion

B] transverse distortion

C] longitudinal distortion

D] distortion due to locked-up stresses

10-75] What is the percentage carbon present in mild steel?

A] 0.05 to 0.1%

B] 0.15 to 0.3%

C] 0.5 to 0.8%

D] 0.8 to 1.4%

INDUSTRIAL TRAINING INSTITUTE

Monthly Test-6, Marks- 20, Date:- ______________

(Every Question Carry Two Marks)

1-81] The name of the part in a DC welding generator which converts the AC supply voltage into DC welding output voltage is...

A] armature

B] commutator

C] field coils

D] carbon brushes

2-82] Which one of the following is the reason for poor fusion of bead with the base metal?

A] electrode travel too slow

B] current too high

C] current too low

D] arc too short

3-83] Which one of the following defects will occurs if the percentage of phosphorus is more in the base metal?

A] slag inclusion

B] surface crack

C] lack of fusion

D] undercut

4-84] Which method of test you will use to check a surface crack on a mild steel welded joint at a cheaper cost?

A] X-ray test

B] ultrasonic test

C] visual inspection

D] magnetic particle test

5-85] Which one of the following defects can be tested found by a Nick Break test on T fillet joint?

A] crater cracks

B] surface cracks

C] lack of root penetration

D] insufficient throat thickness

6-86] Which one of the following metal plates can NOT be joined by projection welding process?

A] tin plates

B] copper plates

C] mild steel plates

D] stainless steel plates

7-87] In which position of pipe welding, the pipe is fixed and inclined at 45? to both horizontal and vertical plane?

A] 1G

B] 2G

C] 5G

D] 6G

8-88] The current to be set for welding a pipe butt joint with a 2.5mmØ rutile coated M.S electrode is...

A] 50A to 70A

B] 70A to 80A

C] 80A to 90A

D] 90A to 100A

9-89] Downhill method of welding of pipe is done while welding

A] a thin walled pipe by rolling

B] a thin walled pipe in fixed position

C] a thick walled pipe by rolling

D] a thick walled pipe in fixed position

10-90] In which pipe welding position all positional welding is required to be done?

A] 1G (Rolling)

B] 2G

C] 5G

D] 1G (segmental)

INDUSTRIAL TRAINING INSTITUTE

Monthly Test-7, Marks- 20, Date:- ______________

(Every Question Carry Two Marks)

1-96] Columbium based stainless steel electrode is used for welding stainless steel joints] The will prevent...

A] Crack in the joint

B] weld decay

C] distortion

D] spatter

2-97] Porosity in stainless steel weld is due to the use of...

A] short arc

B] less current

C] damp electrode

D] unstabilised electrode

3-98] Which one of the following is used in the oxy-arc cutting process?

A] flux coated solid electrode

B] bare wire tubular electrode

C] flux coated tubular electrode

D] bare tungsten arc cutting electrode

4-99] The electrode holder in a carbon arc cutting equipment is made up of...

A] plain carbon steel

B] galvanized iron

C] aluminium

D] copper

5-100] Coping unit of copying lathe is work on

A] Mechanical power system

B] Hand power system

C] Hydraulic power system

D] None of them

6-101] The inner formers of a hydraulic pipe bending machine are able to bend pipes up to a diameter of

A] 40mm

B] 100mm

C] 20mm

D] 75mm

7-102] Which is not the property of hydraulic fluid used in grinding machine?

A] it must not control or absorb air

B] it must not cause corrosion of the moving parts

C] Should have adequate viscosity

D] it must vaporize at the operating temperature

8-103] Which one of the following is the advantage of pneumatic system?

A] For low cost layout

B] For increasing the rate of production

C] For better working environment

9-104] Following which advantage of Pneumatic power system

A] For increase production rate.

B] Less cash for layout

C] Good climate for work

D] Above all

10-105]The pressure of fluid in hydraulic brake system is governed by

A] boils law

B] Charles law

C] Pascal's law

D] none of the above laws

INDUSTRIAL TRAINING INSTITUTE

Monthly Test-8, Marks- 20, Date:- ______________

(Every Question Carry Two Marks)

1-111] Develops pressure on fuel to go out

A] Valves

B] Coil spring

C] Diaphragm

D] Rocker arm

2-112] Actuates the diaphragm

A] Valves

B] Coil spring

C] Diaphragm

D] Rocker arm

3-113] Allow fuel to flow in and out

A] Valves

B] Coil spring

C] Diaphragm

D] Rocker arm

4-114] An overflow valve is used

A] to send back excess fuel from the fuel filler

B] to supply more fuel to the fuel filter

C] to supply clean fuel

D] to take the leaking fuel]

5-115] Excessive oil pressure in the lubrication system may be due to

A] less quantity of engine oil in sump

B] incorrect adjustment of relief valve

C] less suction effect on the suction pipe

D] none of the above

6-116] when oil pressure increases above set limit, oil returns to sump through

A] pressure relief valve

B] by pass valve

C] oil filter

D] oil pump

7-117] Supplies air to front and rear brake

A] Brake actuator

B] Dual brake valve

C] System protection valve

D] Flick valve

8-118] Operated for parking the vehicle]

A] Brake actuator

B] Dual brake valve

C] System protection valve

D] Flick valve

9-119] Exerts spring pressure and applies brake when air pressure in system is less

A] Brake actuator

B] Dual brake valve

C] System protection valve

D] Flick valve

10-120] Distributes air to various circuits

A] Brake actuator

B] Dual brake valve

C] System protection valve

D] Flick valve

INDUSTRIAL TRAINING INSTITUTE

Monthly Test-9, Marks- 20, Date:- ______________

(Every Question Carry Two Marks)

1-126] Starting point of piston's upward movement in the cylinder

A] T.D.C.

B] Cycle

C] B.D.C]

D] Ignition

2-127] Prevents blow by

A] Piston

B] Piston pin

C] Connecting rod

D] Piston rings

3-128] Reciprocates in the cylinder

A] Piston
B] Piston pin
C] Connecting rod
D] Piston rings

4-129] Connects piston and connecting rod
A] Piston
B] Piston pin
C] Connecting rod
D] Piston rings

5-130] Oscillates in cylinder
A] Piston
B] Piston pin
C] Connecting rod
D] Piston rings

6-131] The top and bottom halves of connecting rod are bolted on
A] crankshaft man journal
B] crankpin journal
C] camshaft
D] piston pin boss

7-132] A hole is drilled between crankshaft main journal and crank pin for
A] balancing of crankshaft
B] reducing crankshaft weight
C] lubricating connecting rod bearings
D] reducing crankshaft vibrations

8-133] Relieves excess pressure of air from the air tank]
A] Air compressor
B] Unloader valve
C] Safety valve
D] Brake chamber

9-134] Turns core to magnet
A] Solenoid Switch
B] Actuating wire (when heated)
C] Ballast Resistors
D] Actuating wire (when cooled)

10-135] What is the angle of pipe thread?
A] 60°
B] 47‘/2°

C] 29°

D] 55°]

INDUSTRIAL TRAINING INSTITUTE

Monthly Test-10, Marks- 20, Date:- _______________

(Every Question Carry Two Marks)

1-141]The sealing compound shall be applied on the pipe threads

A] before hemp packing

B] after hemp packing

C] before and after temp packing

D] none of the above.

2-142] Used on finished tubular wrench surfaces to avoid marking]

A Stillson pipe

B] Chain wrench

C] Strap wrench

D] Footprint wrench

3-143] Used for gripping and turning pipes and round stocks in confined places]

A] Stillson pipe

B] Chain wrench

C] Strap wrench

D] Footprint wrench

4-144] Used for holding large diameter pipes]

A] Stillson pipe

B] Chain wrench

C] Strap wrench

D] Footprint wrench

5-145] Used for gripping and turning pipes,tubes and cylindricai rods]

A] Stillson pipe

B] Chain wrench

C] Strap wrench

D] Footprint wrench

6-146] Secures rope to small pipe or rim.

A] Slip knot

B] Bowline knot

C] Square knot

D] Sheep shank knot]

7-147] It can be folded and carried to any place] Similar to the quick releasing type pipe vice.

A Portable folding pipe vice

B] Chain pipe vice

C] Pipe vice

D] None of above

8-148] Used to hold pipes more than 63mm to 200mm diameter.

A] Portable folding pipe vice

B] Chain pipe vice

C] Pipe vice

D] None of above

9-149] Used for quick holding and locating pipes] Used to hold pipes up to 63mm diameter]

A] Portable folding pipe vice

B] Chain pipe vice

C] Pipe vice

D] None of above

10-150] Provides deviation of 90°

A] Plug

B] Elbow

C] Bend

D] Reducer 'T' branczh

INDUSTRIAL TRAINING INSTITUTE

Monthly Test-11, Marks- 20, Date:- ______________

(Every Question Carry Two Marks)

183] Most hydraulic circuits:

a) Operate from a central hydraulic power unit

b) Use air-over-oil power units

c) Have a dedicated power unit

d) Does not have dedicated power unit

184] Hydraulic and pneumatic circuits:

a) Perform the same way for all functions

b) Perform differently for all functions

c) Perform the same with some exceptions

d) Does not perform all the functions

185] The lubricator in a pneumatic circuit is the:

a) First element in line

b) Second element in line

c) Last element in line

d) Third element in line

186] When comparing first cost of hydraulic systems to pneumatic systems, generally they are:

a) More expensive to purchase

b) Less expensive to purchase

c) Cost is same

d) Cost is not required

187] When comparing operating cost of hydraulic systems to pneumatic systems, generally they

are.

a) More expensive to operate

b) Less expensive to operate

c) Cost is same to operate

d) Cost is not required

188] The most common hydraulic fluid is:

a) Mineral oil

b) Synthetic fluid

c) Water

d) Gel

189) Which fluid is used in hydraulic power systems?

a] water

b] oil

c] non-compressible fluid

d] all of the above

190) Pressure of 1 bar is equal to

a] 14]5 psi

b] 145 psi

c] 12]5 psi

d] 145 x 10-6 psi

191) What effect does overloading have on fluid power and electrical systems?

a] electrical components get damaged in electrical systems

b] fluid power system stops working without damaging the components

c] both a] and b]

d] none of the above

192) How is power transmitted in fluid power systems?

a] power is transmitted instantaneously

b] power is transmitted gradually

c] both a] and b]

d] none of the above

INDUSTRIAL TRAINING INSTITUTE

Monthly Test-12, Marks- 20, Date:- _______________

(Every Question Carry Two Marks)

193) Generally liquids are non-compressible but when a large pressure of 70 bar is applied, petroleum oil can be compressed up to

a] 0]5% of its original volume

b] 1% of its original volume

c] 5% of its original volume

d] none of the above

194) The resistance offered to the flow of fluid inside a piston develops into

a] pressure

b] force

c] stress

d] all of the above

195) At low pressures, liquids are

a] compressible

b] non-compressible

c] unpredictable

196) In hydraulic systems,

a] the mechanical energy is transferred to the oil and then converted into mechanical energy

b] the electrical energy is transferred to the oil and then converted into mechanical energy

c] the mechanical energy is transferred to the oil and converted into electrical energy

d] none of the above

197) Which of the following is used as a component in hydraulic power unit?

a] pressure gauge

b] filler gauge

c] valve

d] reservoir

198) Rotary motion in a hydraulic power unit is achieved by using

a] hydraulic cylinder

b] pneumatic cylinder

c] both hydraulic and pneumatic cylinder

d] none of the above

199) What is the relation between speed and flow rate for fixed displacement vane pump?

a] flow rate increases with increase in speed of rotor

b] flow rate decreases with increase in speed of rotor

c] flow rate is constant and does not change with change in speed

d] none of the above

200) In fixed displacement vane pump,

a] flow rate decreases with increase in working pressure

b] flow rate increases with increase in working pressure

c] flow rate is constant and does not change with working pressure

d] none of the above

201) Which type of motion is transmitted by hydraulic actuators?

a] linear motion

b] rotary motion

c] both a] and b]

d] none of the above

202) What is the function of electric actuator?

a] converts electrical energy into mechanical torque

b] converts mechanical torque into electrical energy

c] converts mechanical energy into mechanical torque

d] none of the above

9 798887 041025

Printed by Libri Plureos GmbH in Hamburg,
Germany